Progress in IS

For further volumes:
http://www.springer.com/series/10440

Gianmario Motta · Bing Wu
Editors

Software Engineering Education for a Global E-Service Economy

State of the Art, Trends and Developments

 Springer

Editors
Gianmario Motta
Department of Industrial
    and Information Engineering
University of Pavia
Pavia
Italy

Bing Wu
Department of Computer Science
Dublin Institute of Technology
Dublin
Ireland

ISSN 2196-8705   ISSN 2196-8713 (electronic)
ISBN 978-3-319-04216-9   ISBN 978-3-319-04217-6 (eBook)
DOI 10.1007/978-3-319-04217-6
Springer Cham Heidelberg New York Dordrecht London

Library of Congress Control Number: 2014930227

Printed on acid-free paper

Springer is part of Springer Science+Business Media (www.springer.com)

The China–Europe International Symposium on Software Engineering Education (CEISEE'2013)

International Program Committee

General Chairs
Gianmario Motta (Italy)
Bing Wu (Ireland)

Co-Chairs
Xiaofei Xu (China)
Carlo Batini (Italy)

International Program Committee Members

Vincent Barra (France)
Kamal Bechkoum (UK)
Roberto Bellini (Italy)
Jean-Paul Bourrieres (France)
Huiyou Chang (China)
David Chen (France)
Chuanbo Chen (China)
Deren Chen (China)
Shuyu Chen (China)
Gino Colazzo (Italy)
Shengchun Deng (China)
Yves Ducq (France)
John Dunnion (Ireland)
Marco Ferretti (Italy)
Chiara Francalanci (Italy)
Yuxi Fu (China)
Carlo Ghezzi (Italy)
Kun-Mean Hou (France)
Liang Hu (China)

Matthew Hussey (Ireland)
Mariam Kamkar (Sweden)
Stephan Kassel (Germany)
Patrick Lambrix (Sweden)
Michel Leonhardt (Switzerland)
Minghong Liao (China)
Qin Liu (China)
Wei Lu (China)
Peijun Ma (China)
Andrea Maurino (Italy)
Henry McLoughlin (Ireland)
Xiangxu Meng (China)
Brendan O'Shea (Ireland)
Giulio Occhini (Italy)
Barbara Pernici (Italy)
Mauro Pezzè (Italy)
Raul Poler (Spain)
Lei Qin (China)
Zhiguang Qin (China)
Alain Quilliot (France)
Clive Rosen (UK)
Paolo Schgor (Italy)
Scott Turner (UK)
Gianluigi Viscusi (Italy)
Zhenyu Wang (China)
Bo Wu (China)
Zhonghai Wu (China)
Binyu Zang (China)
Ming Zeng (China)
Li Zhang (China)
Zhiliang Zhu (China)

Organization Committee

Chairs
Gianmario Motta (Italy)
Carlo Batini (Italy)

Members
Dave Carroll (Ireland)
Mara Molinari (Italy)
Ciaran O'Leary (Ireland)
Giulio Occhini (Italy)
Daniele Sacco (Italy)
Gianluigi Viscusi (Italy)

Organizers
University of Pavia, Italy

Co-Organizers
AICA
Politecnico di Milano
Università Milano Bicocca

Main Sponsor
IBM Italy

Sponsors
Harbin Institute of Technology (HIT), China
Dublin Institute of Technology (DIT), Ireland

Supported by
Ministry of Education (MOE), China
Enterprise Ireland, Ireland
European Virtual Laboratory for Enterprise
Interoperability (China Pole)

CEISEE Objectives

The History of China–Europe International Symposium on Software Engineering Education

The China–Europe International Symposium on Software Engineering Education (CEISEE) was evolved from the China–Europe International Symposium on Software Industry Oriented Education (CEISIE), which was founded in 2005, according to rapid development of software engineering education in both China and Europe.

The China–Europe International Symposium on Software Industry Oriented Education was initialized from an international education project, EMERSION project (Education to Meet the Requirements of Software Industry and Beyond—Establishing, Implementing and Evaluating an Industry Oriented Education Model in China), which is supported by the "Asia-Link Programme" of European Commission, with the collaboration of Dublin Institute of Technology (DIT) in Ireland, Harbin Institute of Technology (HIT) in China and University of Wolverhampton (UOW) in the United Kingdom. During the EMERSION project, the project members would like to share the educational achievements and experience with more universities and institutes in Europe and in China.

In January 2005, launched by the members of the EMERSION project, the 1st China–Europe International Symposium on Software Industry Oriented Education was held in HIT, Harbin in China. The initial short name of the symposium was CEIS-SIOE. In January 2006, the 2nd CIES-SIOE was again held in HIT, Harbin. In that conference, it was decided that this conference should be held every year in exchanged sides of either China or Europe. Then the 3rd China–Europe International Symposium on Software Industry Oriented Education was held in DIT, Dublin in Ireland, in February 2007. The initial short name of the symposium was changed from CEIS-SIOE to CEISIE. The 4th CEISIE symposium was held in Sun Yat-Sen University, Guangzhou in China, in January 2008. The 5th CEISIE symposium was held in University of Bordeaux 1, Bordeaux in France, in May 2009. The 6th CEISIE symposium took place in Northwestern Polytechnical University, Xi'an in China, in May 2010. The 7th CEISIE symposium was held in University of Northampton, Northampton in UK, in May 2011. Then it was decided to change the name of the symposium from CEISIE to CEISEE (China–Europe International symposium on Software Engineering Education), in order to extend the scopes of the conference and to emphasize the development of discipline on software engineering. The 8th CEISEE symposium was held in Shanghai Jiaotong University, Shanghai in China, in May 2012.

The CEISIE/CEISEE symposiums have been very successful and attracted great attention from educators, industrialists, and governmental officers, who are interested in software engineering education, across China and Europe. Until now, more than 570 participants from 16 countries, e.g., China, Ireland, UK, France, Germany, Italy, Spain, Switzerland, Sweden, Finland, Poland, Russia, USA, Australia, Tanzania, and South Korea have attended the symposiums.

The CEISEE aims at exploring new approaches to develop the software engineering discipline and software engineering education in both China and Europe, according to the changing tendency of technical development of software engineering and educational requirements of the software talents all over the world. The CEISEE is a good platform for educators, industrialists, and government officers related to software engineering education to exchange their ideas, to share their experience, and to develop their academic community in this domain.

CEISEE 2013: Topics

The 9th CEISEE symposium was held in Milan, Italy, in May 2013. It was organized by the University of Pavia. Pavia is among the oldest European universities, and it was founded in 1361 by the Duke of Milan. Differently from most Italian universities, Pavia is a University city, with 25 colleges and student halls, like Oxford or Cambridge. The University of Pavia has been always ranked among the top Italian universities, and had Professors such as Volta (the inventor of the electric pile), Cardano (the inventor of the cardanic joint and of cubic equations), Golgi (a Nobel Prize in Medicine), etc. In cooperation with Pavia, the symposium was organized by the University of Milano Bicocca, the youngest university in Milan, founded in 1998, and Politecnico di Milano, the largest technical university in Italy, founded some 100 years ago. The symposium was hosted by AICA, the Italian Society for Information Technology, which is associated to ACM.

The theme of CEISEE 2013 was *Software Engineering Education for Global E-Service Economy*. In general terms, the topics of CEISEE 2013 included:

- Education model for software engineering
- Development of discipline on software engineering
- Innovation and evaluation of software engineering education
- Curriculum for software engineering education
- Requirement and cultivation of outstanding software engineers for the future
- Cooperation model for industries and software engineering education
- Internationalization of software engineering education
- Education for service science and engineering
- Software engineering education for global e-services economics

- Quality assurance and evaluation in software engineering education
- E-Learning and support tools for software education
- Course development for software engineering, Internet of things, Internet of services, service science and engineering, ICT application for enterprises
- Certification and authentication for professional education on software engineers
- Interdisciplinary education in Service Science, Management of Information Systems, Quality of Services, and Systems.

CEISEE 2013: Summary of the Keynote Speech and Panel

The keynote speaker, Prof. Carlo Ghezzi from Politecnico di Milano, a world known authority in Software Engineering addressed "Informatics education in Europe," covering Informatics education in High school up to universities. The key assumptions for a better informatics education in the future rely on the following points. First, students should be challenged to work in modern project settings, and this is not just a question of using modern technology; a modern project setting implies for instance to work with teams scattered around the world with a service-oriented architecture. In teaching, durable principles should be emphasized as well as the use of modern technology. Finally, it is desperately needed to form citizens of the future who will lead to a wealthy innovative society.

The subsequent panel addressed the requirements of industry versus the education models; it was made of top industry representative (demand), which included ENI and IBM, and university/school representatives (supply), as HIT (founder of CEISEE), Politecnico di Milano (the largest Italian technical university), and AICA (the Italian Society for Information Technology).

Mr. Castelli, CIO of ENI, pointed out the challenges of the Software/Systems Engineer job in a very large corporation. A challenge is the complexity of a corporation with over 500 applications, where new and old applications must coexist and cooperate, therefore requiring an all-round expert, who is able also to program and to understand programs. This leads to a set of recommendations—back to basics, learn Knuth's Art of computer programming, develop the ability of integrating systems.

Mr. Morucci, from the Rome IBM Software Lab, considered the abilities of software/systems engineers in IBM, certainly one of the largest IT services organizations. He underlined that the careers of software/system engineer grow on different tracks, that include Consulting, Technical Services, Architect, and IT Specialist, and, finally, Software/Hardware Engineer. All career paths can eventually lead to the executive level, called "IBM fellow".

Professor XU from Harbin Institute of Technology (HIT), founder of CEISEE, discussed the perspectives and issues in China of industry oriented software engineering education. This led in 2003 to National Pilot Professional Schools of Software, that nowadays count some 200 university programs.

Professor Pernici, from Politecnico di Milano, illustrated the objectives of the Politecnico's Doctoral School.

Finally Prof. Bellini, President of AICA Milano, presented the approach of Council of European Professionals Informatics Societies (CEPIS) and AICA (the Italian Society for Information Technology) on post-graduated education, based on a set of standard competence frameworks, for computer literacy, ICT practitioners, and e-citizens. Specifically, the EUCIP system (for ICT practitioners), active since middle 2000, addresses 155 competences clustered in some 30 practitioner profiles. EUCIP releases a certification and also an assessment of individual competences.

CEISEE 2013: Papers

The papers presented in the Symposium have been grouped in tracks, respectively:

- Techniques and Technologies for Software Engineering Education
- Software Engineering Education versus Industry Demand
- Curricula for Software Engineering Education

The first track targets the tools that a professor uses in teaching software engineering. It is a classic track of CEISEE, that presents and assesses teaching approaches as e-Learning, the use of natural language to teach compilers, the certification of authenticity, and, finally, the autonomy of old people.

The second track considers a topic that has also been addressed by the panel, namely the requirements of the demand—i.e., the industry—versus the structure of the offer supplied by universities. There you can find case studies of specific Master curricula that are conceived to optimize the quality of the outcome; not surprisingly, they use a blend of academic professors and practice professors. This strong industry orientation is led, at least in China, by the industry orientation of software schools, while research is mainly in Computer Engineering curricula.

Also in the third track, more targeted on curricula, the search for a strong and effective industry link is a recurring point. Some papers also address the relationship between software engineering and service science.

Contents

Part I
Techniques and Technologies for Software Engineering Education

E-learning for Employability: A Case Study from a UK Master's Programme

Jenny Carter and Ian Pettit

Abstract The MSc Intelligent Systems (IS) and the MSc Intelligent Systems and Robotics (ISR) programmes at De Montfort University are Masters level courses that are delivered both on-site and by distance learning. The courses have been running successfully on-site for 8 years and are now in the fifth year with a distance learning mode. Delivering material at a distance, especially where there is technical and practical content, presents a challenge and in this chapter we focus on some of the techniques adopted to overcome these challenges. The second focus of the chapter is the reasons why the students choose to study such a course and the implications they believe it has on their future employability.

Keywords Post-graduate · E-learning · Employability

1 Introduction

The MSc Intelligent Systems (IS) and the MSc Intelligent Systems and Robotics (ISR) programmes at De Montfort University are Masters level courses that are delivered both on-site and by distance learning (DL). The courses are delivered mainly by the members of the Centre for Computational Intelligence (CCI) at De Montfort University. Their development enabled us to capitalise on the research taking place within the CCI and therefore on the strengths of the staff delivering the modules.

J. Carter (✉)
Centre for Computational Intelligence, Faculty of Technology, De Montfort University,
Leicester, UK
e-mail: jennyc@dmu.ac.uk

I. Pettit
Centre for Enhancing Learning through Technology, Library and Learning Services,
De Montfort University, Leicester, UK
e-mail: ipettit@dmu.ac.uk

G. Motta and B. Wu (eds.), *Software Engineering Education for a Global
E-Service Economy*, Progress in IS, DOI: 10.1007/978-3-319-04217-6_1,
© Springer International Publishing Switzerland 2014

Each MSc consists of 8 taught modules and an independent project which is equivalent to 4 modules. Each module is worth 15 credits (7.5 ECTS). The MSc ISR includes two mobile robots modules whilst MSc IS replaces one of these with a Data Mining module as an alternative application area for those less interested in pursuing mobile robotics work. A Research Methods module is delivered in semester 1 to ensure that students are equipped with the necessary skills to carry out literature searches, write project proposals and so on; and a module titled 'Applied Computational Intelligence (CI)' enables students to pursue an appropriate area of their own interest in greater depth. An overview of the course content is shown in Fig. 1. In this chapter we discuss the issues associated with delivering such a course at a distance and investigate the motivation of the students for embarking on such a programme. In this part we particularly consider the employability of the students.

The remainder of the chapter is structured as follows: Sect. 2 discusses approaches to learning on the MSc programmes and how this fits with recognised approaches from the associated literature; Sect. 3 considers the e-learning provision in the Faculty of Technology; Sect. 4 provides a discussion of the students' perceptions of the course both in terms of its delivery and the perceived benefits on completion; and Sect. 5 draws conclusions from this work.

2 Approaches to Learning

In order to deliver the course effectively it has been useful to consider approaches to learning and teaching in higher education more generally. Most of the modules include both theoretical and practical work and the assessments are usually open enough to allow the students to investigate appropriate topics in their own way thus there is an attempt to facilitate experiential learning as defined by Kolb [1]. We believe it to be very important for our students to draw on non-course experiences as many of them have work experience: for example, DL students are often in full time employment, there is a wide variety of first degree subjects amongst them and some already have PhDs.

We aim to adopt an approach to our delivery of the courses that embraces modern technology in such a way that the students have appropriate learning experiences whether they are studying on-site or at a distance.

The Quality Assurance Agency (QAA) for Higher education in the UK provides codes of practice for all types of learning. There is a section of the documentation that is aimed specifically at flexible and distributed learning and within this they include e-learning [2]. These codes of practice are observed by all higher education institutions in the United Kingdom and there are government led procedures in place to monitor their appropriate application. Precepts are stated in the QAA documentation that define what the students should be able to expect from their institution, their learning materials, their tutors and so on when engaged in flexible, distance or electronic learning.

Fig. 1 The course structure

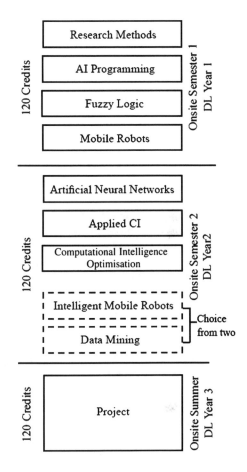

One area of attention identified by the QAA in [3] is that of formative feedback, where students are given feedback on their work but that feedback does not relate to any marks or grades for the course or module. One of the ways that we address this is by using regular discussion board activity; this is described more fully in [4]. Another area of attention to highlight is that of plagiarism detection and prevention. We adopt various strategies for this including the use of TurnitinUK for checking authenticity and the use of vivas or presentations/demonstrations using Skype. The discussion board is also a substantial aid in both prevention and detection. In addition to this we set assignments that can be approached in a variety of ways, which reduces the opportunity for students to work too closely together. Prevention and detection of plagiarism is beyond the scope of the work presented here so will not be addressed further.

The QAA suggest that excessive amounts of summative assessment should be avoided. They state that "it is good practice to provide students with sufficient, constructive and timely feedback on their work" [2, p. 20] and this is an area that we have addressed recently. Timing has been an issue on our course as there has been a significant delay before the students receive their marked work. This is no longer the case and our approach to the solution of this is described fully in [5].

De Montfort University already uses Blackboard as a platform for providing e-learning materials for all students and this is used extensively though not exhaustively in all faculties. It was therefore an obvious choice as the main platform for the MSc. Decisions about the best way to use Blackboard and which other resources to employ alongside it were necessary and as both on-site and distance students study the modules concurrently, the experiences need to be as similar as possible.

Some practices have been adopted for all modules and this includes providing some physical materials (e.g. software). We also record lectures and post them on De Montfort University's streaming server; they can then be viewed as streamed video through Blackboard and it has proved to be a popular method. Other methods adopted include sound over Powerpoint slides using tools such as Articulate Presenter and more recently Microsoft Expression Encoder. We also provide software demonstrations using screen and voice recorders.

Assignments are made available to students on Blackboard and they are asked to submit them to Blackboard for electronic marking. The students submit their work twice, once to TurnitinUK and once to an assignment submission link. This work is then marked using electronic methods and the annotated scripts with provisional marks are posted in a feedback space on Blackboard that is generated when the students submit their work. Multiple files can be uploaded to this space both by students and the marking tutors. This means that the students get feedback as soon as the work is marked.

As well as the need for feedback to be timely it also needs to be of a high quality in order for learners to be able to use it to determine further actions. This is identified in case study 4 of the Joint Information Systems Committee [JISC] [6] which states that "feedback must:

- Be helpful, detailed and appropriate to learners' current understanding
- Provide more detail with each failed attempt
- Identify a means of rectifying errors
- Invite an active response" [6, p. 1].

The report emphasises the particular importance of this with respect to DL students. Adding quality to feedback is also highlighted by Clark and Meyer [7] where studies are described that show that explanatory feedback resulted in improved learning compared with the effects of corrective feedback; explanatory feedback being where some explanation is given in the feedback when something is incorrect. The authors in [7] also go on to state that such explanations ideally should be succinct and positioned so that they are close physically to where the error in the students' work took place. Other studies, notably [8, 9], also promote explanatory feedback by referring to it as descriptive and emphasising how it provides useful information to enable the gap to be filled between the current student performance and the desired performance. In order to offer good quality courses we aim to provide appropriate feedback that adheres to the codes of practise identified by the QAA and promotes students learning as described in the previous paragraphs.

The methods adopted for assessing the electronic submissions vary. Most tutors make use of a marking grid, an example of which is shown in Fig. 2 and some staff provide summary feedback to go with the annotated grid. In such cases this forms the entire feedback and can be made available quickly. Most tutors prefer to write comments on the students' work in addition to the use of a marking grid and it is this that has posed problems in the past for returning the feedback in a timely manner. Staff now all have a pen tablet for annotating scripts electronically. With such software as Acrobat Professional, annotations on the students work can be carried out by using the typewriter tool, by hand-writing comments using the pen-tablet, by inserting electronic sticky notes or even by adding voice recordings. The number of different ways of adding feedback electronically enabled by providing this software and hardware has meant that all staff have adopted one of the electronic methods described. In [5] two modules used electronic methods for assessment and feedback as a pilot study and students opinions of the change were gathered in by means of a short survey. The results showed that all students preferred this method, even the on-site students. These results are fully reported in [5].

A consideration during the development of the course was the idea of networked learning. Goodyear et al. [10] define the term 'networked learning' to describe a particular kind of web-based or on-line learning. Their definition of networked learning is "learning in which information and communications technology is used to promote connections: between one learner and other learners; between learners and tutors; between a learning community and its resources". It is important for us to make sure that we are not simply providing materials in a variety of forms but that the learning is networked i.e. there is human to human communication taking place within each module.

One way that we do this is to make use of an assessed discussion board on our virtual learning environment (VLE). It is assessed based on the number of contributions over the semester rather than the quality of the content. We have found this to be very successful and it is clear that it helps to create a virtual learning community amongst our students.

Such communities are identified as being important for student engagement in e-learning by Dabbagh [11]. Our experience of using this mechanism has shown that it encourages students to become more of a cohort through communicating with each other whether on-site or at a distance and it helps the distance students in particular to feel less isolated. The discussion board component is worth 10 % on every module and it is this that encourages students to use it initially. We find that as they get used to using it they become more involved and often answer each other's questions and so on. Other practises used, though to a lesser extent, are blogs, which are used for keeping project journals and also as a way of putting current students in touch with past graduates from the course; a Facebook group; and more recently wikis for sharing subject related ideas and student presentations.

Marking scheme for essay/report – worth 60% of overall mark

	0 – 44% Fail	45-49% Marginal Fail	50-54% Pass	55-59% Pass	60-69% Merit	>70% Distinction
Coverage of area, including literature review.	Not acceptable	Some attempt to cover the area but with serious limitations.	Brief with significant limitations.	Good coverage, but with some notable limitations.	Very good coverage of area and associated issues with good review of literature.	Excellent coverage, showing a sound understanding of topic. Excellent critical review of literature.
Practical (e.g. implementation or experimental work)	Very little of value	Weak, with substantial limitations. Some effort evident.	Satisfactory amount of work. Significant limitations in design & documentation.	Good work, with some limitations.	Very good work, very good documentation and design. Only minor limitations	Challenging work, well documented, well designed
Conclusions, recommendations, critical evaluation, new ideas, etc.	Missing or poor or not meaningful	A minimal attempt with serious limitations. Not acceptable.	Satisfactory but with significant limitations.	Good, but with some notable limitations. Lacks depth.	Very good, comprehensive, with good ideas.	Excellent, follows logically from body of report and contains excellent and original ideas.
Structure and presentation. References, bibliography.	No clear structure, and presentation very weak. Poor or no bibliography, reference list, citations in report.	Weak structure poor presentation. Poor bibliography, reference list, citations in report.	Satisfactory approach to structure and presentation. List of references present but with significant limitations.	Well structured and presentation good. Most references in correct format from both web and traditional sources.	Very well structured and prepared with only minor limitations. References cited in correct notation from both web and traditional sources.	Highly professional approach; excellent structure. Thorough reference citation from a variety of sources.

Fig. 2 Example of marking grid

The next section focuses on how facilities for e-learning provision are being developed in the wider context within the Faculty of Technology and the university as a whole.

3 E-learning Provision in the Faculty of Technology

This section looks at E-learning provision in the Faculty of Technology. In September 2011 De Montfort University created the Centre for Enhancing Learning through Technology (CELT) in order to take a consistent and supportive approach to ELT in the curriculum. The centre comprises of seven staff members; the Head of CELT and six Project Officers, four of whom are based in the Faculties at DMU. The centre is part of the Library and Learning Services Directorate and links closely with the Academic Professional Development Unit by way of providing support and staff development activities in the field of ELT.

Within the Faculty of Technology, the assigned CELT Project Officer works to identify and document good practice for dissemination and to support staff members in fully exploiting the situated technology, whether that is technology specifically for ELT or technology that has been provided by the central Information, Technology and Media Services (ITMS) team. There is a close relationship between ITMS and the CELT as ITMS will source and supply technology as the responsibility for provision and technical support lies with this team, however the CELT has a remit to ensure that, where pedagogically appropriate, technology that has been provided by ITMS is used to support the curriculum and to enhance the student experience fully.

Outside of this more formal arrangement, DMU does encourage staff and students to innovate the teaching and learning experience by experimenting with new and different technologies as the curriculum evolves and needs change. Part of the CELT's responsibility is to support this organic growth of innovation by acting as a critical friend and expert user in order to help test new technologies and identify and document the potential benefits or otherwise of introducing a new technology into the curriculum.

This blend of a formal agreement to support the use of situated technology in the curriculum along with encouraging experimentation with new technologies works well and is in line with the 'Core, Arranged, Recommended, Recognised' model [12] as developed by Manchester Metropolitan University and adopted by DMU.

The MSc Intelligent Systems (IS) and the MSc Intelligent Systems and Robotics (ISR) programmes showcase the way in which the CELT works to identify and share good practice and support the further innovation of teaching methods.

The good practice involving electronic marking techniques and the use of assessed Discussion Boards was documented and disseminated in spring 2012. These elements were documented by the CELT Project Officer working with the Faculty of Technology and twelve months on other staff from around the university are considering adopting these approaches for both distance learners and attending students.

During the conversations with the teaching team, other areas where technology may help to enhance the curriculum further were identified and these are being investigated at the time of writing. Such initiatives include the potential to use 3D printers to create bespoke parts for the robots in order to promote more hands on and practical activities.

The CELT is working toward the implementation of an online hub where all of the content and resources that the CELT produces will be available on the open web for re-purposing and sharing. This hub is due to be online in February 2013. In the meantime, for further information about the Centre for Enhancing Learning through Technology please visit the DMU Learning Exchanges website [12].

The next section provides a discussion of the students' perceptions of the course both in terms of its delivery and the perceived benefits on completion.

4 Student Perceptions

In order to find out more about the students' perspective on the course a questionnaire was sent out to 59 on-site and distance students. 15 were completed and returned at the time of writing this chapter. The aim of the questionnaire was to find out the opinions of the students about the different materials that they are presented with and additionally to find out why they chose to do the course and what they hope to achieve in terms of their employability as a result of completing it.

All of the respondents to the questionnaire found out about the course through the internet and almost all of them chose to do it for either both of or one of the two same reasons, namely: career enhancement and personal interest. All of them are interested in doing research as part of or during the MSc and all but one are interested in continuing to study for a PhD. Many of our past students have gone on to do PhDs, some on-site, some in other institutions and some as distance learners.

When asked about the quality of the materials provided, there was generally positive feedback and they particularly like the videos and the sound over slides. There is still room for improvement however, as one or two modules do not offer this. The quality of some of the videos was an issue as well though the poorer quality videos have now all been replaced.

Almost all students said that they find the discussion board useful. Negative comments related to particular modules where tutor responses or feedback had not taken place regularly. Few of the respondents use the Facebook group or the e-community on Blackboard. However, evidence from Facebook itself shows that some students do use it and it also attracts past students which enables us to maintain links with graduates from the course.

Thirteen of the respondents are employed and all work in the IT field. Some see the course as a means to change direction in their employment e.g. "I hope to put it to use in the future, maybe a new job or a research position" whereas others see it as a way to develop within their current role "I expect to be able to find new solutions to problems", another student works with trading models in finance and wants to apply Computational Intelligence techniques to solve problems within that industry. Another student said "I run my own company (software) and I would like to expand (more services and products)".

A pleasing finding is that most students agreed that they felt a sense of belonging on the MSc (10) and only 2 said that they did not. Most people do not feel isolated while studying on the course though a small number do.

5 Conclusions

In this chapter we have described the MSc in Intelligent Systems and MSc Intelligent Systems and Robotics. As courses that runs both on-site and by distance learning, they are often used as an example in our own institution.

Delivering courses at a distance is a topical area. With the many available mechanisms for interacting with learners electronically there are a number of choices to be made regarding the approach to take. In this chapter we have described some of the approaches taken to the delivery of the learning materials and our approaches to assessment and feedback. We have also described the introduction of the CELT at De Montfort University and the Faculty of Technology's own CELT Project Officer. These are valuable assets that support the development of e-learning both in terms of trying and testing appropriate technologies but also addressing pedagogic issues that arise when delivering distance and e-materials.

Opinions about the material and the delivery methods have been gathered from students along with some information regarding their reasons for doing the course and the perceived subsequent impact on employability and career development. The students' opinions about the course are generally very positive, as are their perceptions of it as an aid to career development. The survey has highlighted some issues on a module by module basis and has given us some detailed information to work with.

The course is successful and sustainable with a total of 59 students currently enrolled (5 on site, the rest as distance learning). It continues to evolve as the available technologies improve; we continue to gather feedback regularly, using the responses to inform future developments. We hope to continue in this way ensuring that our students benefit from a carefully crafted course that makes appropriate use of current e-learning research and associated technology.

References

1. Kolb, D. (1984). *Experiential learning: Experience as the source of learning and development*. New Jersey: Prentice-Hall
2. QA codes of Practice, Section 2. (2010) [Online] http://www.qaa.ac.uk/academicinfra-structure/codeofpractice/default.asp
3. QA codes of Practice, Section 6. (2006) [Online] http://www.qaa.ac.uk/academicinfra-structure/codeofpractice/default.asp
4. Carter, J., & Coupland, S. (2010). Teaching robotics at the postgraduate level: delivering for on site and distance learning. In *Proceedings of the International Conference on Robotics in Education (RIE2010)*.
5. Carter, J., Matthews, S., & Coupland, S. (2011). Teaching robotics at the postgraduate level: assessment & feedback for on site and distance learning. In *Proceedings of the International Conference on Robotics in Education (RIE2011)*.

6. JISC. (2010) [Online] Designing interactive assessments to promote independent learning, http://www.jisc.ac.uk/media/documents/programmes/elearning/digiassess_interactiveassessments.pdf

7. Clark, R., & Meyer R. E. (2008). *E-learning & the science of instruction*. New York: Wiley.

8. Nicol, D. J., & Milligan, C. (2006). Rethinking technology-supported assessment in terms of the seven principles of good feedback practice. In C. Bryan & K. Clegg (Eds.), *Innovative assessment in higher education*. London: Taylor and Francis Group Ltd.

9. Wiggins, G. (2001). *Educative assessment*. San Francisco: Jossey-Bass.

10. Goodyear, P., Banks, S., Hodgson, V, & McConnell, D. (2008). *Advances in research on networked learning* (pp. 1–10). New York: Springer.

11. Dabbagh, N. (2005). Pedagogical models for e-learning: A theory-based design framework. *International Journal of Technology in Teaching and Learning, 1*, 25–44.

12. http://www.learnex.dmu.ac.uk/e-learningdmu/dmu-core-technologies

Introducing Natural Language Examples in a Course on Compiler Principles

Yin Chen

Abstract "Compiler principles" is widely regarded as the most difficult specialized course in software engineering major because of its difficult theory and abstract content. This chapter discusses how to introduce natural language examples into the classroom teaching, and therefore liberate students from abstract theory explanation.

Keywords Compiler principles · Classroom teaching · Natural language

1 Introduction

"Compiler principles" is an important specialized course of software engineering major. It is commonly regarded as the most difficult course to teach and learn because of its difficult theory and abstract content. So teachers should give some intuitional examples to students for better understanding. This chapter introduces some natural language examples into the course compiler principles. Natural language, which is relative to programming language, refers to the language people use in daily life. It is the language of human society, and is the language people most familiar with. In fact, programming language is built on the abstraction of natural language. The manners computer analyzes and processes programming language are similar to the manners people understand and use natural language. So, it couldn't be better if we use natural language examples in course teaching.

Y. Chen (✉)
School of Software, Harbin Institute of Technology, Harbin, China
e-mail: chenyin@hit.edu.cn

G. Motta and B. Wu (eds.), *Software Engineering Education for a Global E-Service Economy*, Progress in IS, DOI: 10.1007/978-3-319-04217-6_2,
© Springer International Publishing Switzerland 2014

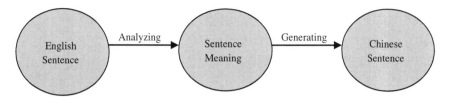

Fig. 1 English-Chinese translation process

This chapter attempts to introduce natural language examples into the course. Two examples shown in this chapter demonstrate that this method can liberate students from the abstract theory explanation.

2 A Natural Language Example in Course Introduction

In theory, compiling process usually includes five stages, which are lexical analysis, syntax analysis, semantic analysis, codes optimization and target code generation. This is usually the content teachers narrate in the course introduction. It is not difficult for students to memorize these five stages, but it is a little difficult for them to understand the dividing evidence for these stages. Teachers should advocate students to memorize based on understanding. Students need to know not only what it is, but also why it is so.

The main task of Compiler is to translate the source program written in programming language into equivalent target program written in machine language or assemble language. Since compiling essentially is a translation process, its working process is similar to foreign language translation. The only difference is that source language and target language are different [1].

Now, let us see what steps will be needed if we translate the English sentence "In the room, he broke a window with a hammer." into Chinese (we may adopt heuristic method in course teaching which requests students themselves to think and summarize).

Generally, the translating procedure includes two steps (see Fig. 1). Firstly, we need to analyze the meaning of the source language (English) sentence which is called semantics. Next, we construct equivalent target language (Chinese) sentence based on the given semantics. The first step can be called "analysis procedure" which is from source language to semantics, this procedure only involves source language, but is independent of target language. The second step can be called "generating procedure" which is from semantics to target language, this procedure only involves target language, but is independent of source language. So, semantics is an intermedia which is independent of concrete language.

Analysis process can be further divided into several steps. Generally speaking, apart from core predicate verb, a sentence also includes some noun components,

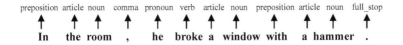

Fig. 2 Lexical analysis of the sentence

which are called entities. The essence of semantic analysis is to determine the relationship between these noun components and the core predicate verb. These relationships are called "case" in linguistics, including agentive case, dative case, time case, locative case, instrumental case, etc. Therefore, for a complex sentence, in order to acquire its meaning, we should firstly identify the core predicate verb and noun components in the sentence; in order to identify these components, we should firstly analyze the sentence structure (this process is called "syntax analysis"); in order to analyze the sentence structure, we should firstly determine the part-of-speech of each word in the sentence (this process is called "lexical analysis"). So, the analysis process can be further divided into three steps, which are lexical analysis, syntax analysis and semantic analysis.

For the above example, after lexical analysis, we get part of speech sequence corresponding to the sentence as shown in Fig. 2.

Next, according to English grammar, we get the structure of this sentence as shown in Fig. 3. According to the syntax analysis result, we can identify the core predicate verb and noun phrases in the sentence.

Next, we would analyze the sentence's meaning according to semantic rules. In linguistics, case grammar [2] is used to express the semantic concept in the deep structure of grammar system. Case grammar is a linguistic theory proposed by the American linguist Fillmore in 1966 [3]. Simply put, the case grammar can be regarded as grammar with case. For example, if the English case grammar has such a semantic rule as shown in Fig. 4.

Then, we can get the meaning of the above English sentence. That is, the core event described by the sentence is "break", the agent of this event is "he", the object of this event is "a window", the instrumental used in the event is "a hammer", location of the event is "In the room". Semantic results of case grammar may be expressed by case framework. For example, the semantic analysis result of the above sentence is represented by the following case framework.

[break

  [case-frame

    agent: he
    object: a window
    locative: in the room
    instrument: a hammer

  ]
  [modals

Fig. 3 Syntax analysis of the sentence

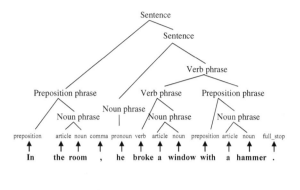

Fig. 4 Example for semantic rule

sentence → in-phrase + noun-phrase + break + noun-phrase + with-phrase

Location   Agent   Object   Instrument

time: past
voice: active

]

]

Now the analysis process has been accomplished, and the generating process is just opposite process to the analysis process, which constructs the structure of the Chinese (target language) sentence and the concrete word sequence, based on the case frame.

In fact, the principle of compiler is similar to translation process. It is also divided into these stages as lexical analysis, syntax analysis, semantic analysis and target code generation. Their difference lies in the following aspects:

1. In English-Chinese translation, the task of lexical analysis is to determine the type of each word in the sentence. Here, word type refers to part-of-speech including nouns, verbs, adjectives, prepositions, pronouns, adverbs, etc.; The task of compiler's lexical analysis is also to recognize words and words' types in the source program. However, word's type here includes keyword, identifier, operator, bounded symbol, constant etc.

2. In English-Chinese translation, the task of syntax analysis is to analyze the structure of English sentence, and to identify the core predicate verb and noun components; However, the task of compiler's syntax analysis is to analyze structure of program language (source language)'s sentence, and to identify the key part (such as "var", "proc", ":=", "if", "else", "switch", "while", "for", "call") and other components of the sentence.

3. In English-Chinese translation, the task of semantic analysis is to determine the relationship between each noun component and the core predicate of English sentence based on semantic rules (case grammar), and therefore represent the

Table 1 Analogy between English-Chinese translation and compiling process

	English-Chinese translation	Compiling
Lexical analysis	Determine part-of-speech (nouns, verbs, adjectives, prepositions, pronouns, adverbs, etc.) of each word in English sentence	Recognize words and words' types (keywords, identifiers, operator, bounded symbol, constant etc.) in source program
Syntax analysis	Analyze the structure of English sentence, and identify the core predicate verb and noun components	Analyze structure of program language's sentence, and identify the key part (such as "var", "proc", ":=", "if", "else", "switch", "while", "for", "call") and other components of the sentence
Semantic analysis	Determine the relationship between each noun components and the core predicate of english sentence based on semantic rules (case grammar), and therefore represent the analysis result by case framework	Transfer the source program into intermediate code according to syntax-directed definitions (SDD)
Target code generation	Construct Chinese sentence's structure and the concrete word sequence based on case frame	Generate machine language or assembly language program according to intermediate code

analysis result by case framework; However, the task of compiler's semantic analysis is to transfer the source program into intermediate code (such as three address instruction) according to syntax-directed definitions (SDD). Similarly to case framework, intermediate code has fixed format and is independent of concrete language. In three address instruction, the operator is corresponding to the core predicate verb of natural language sentence, and each operand (source, target) is corresponding to various case of core predicate verb.

4. In English-Chinese translation, the task of generating process is to construct Chinese (target language) sentence's structure and the concrete word sequence based on case frame; However, the task of compiler's generating process is to generate machine language or assembly language program according to intermediate code.

The above analogical processes are summarized in Table 1. Through the analogy between compiler's stages and natural language translation process, students can deeply understand the dividing evidence for compiler's stages, and thus better understand the working process of compiler.

3 A Natural Language Example in "Handle" Teaching and Learning

"Handle" is also an abstract concept in learning process of students. The key problem of bottom-up analysis is how to correctly recognize handle. Simply put, handle is the symbol string that should be reduced each time in bottom-up analysis process. Handle is the body (right part) of a production. In the LR analysis method, handle is defined as "left-most direct phrase". "Left" is easy for students to understand, so the key problem is how to correctly identify direct phrase. According to the definition of a direct phrase—assuming $S \Rightarrow {}^*\alpha\gamma\beta$ (i.e. $\alpha\gamma\beta$ is sentence pattern), if $S \Rightarrow {}^*\alpha A\beta$, and $A \Rightarrow \gamma$ (i.e. $A \rightarrow \gamma \in P$), then γ is called direct phrase of sentence pattern $\alpha\gamma\beta$ corresponding to variable A—it can be seen that direct phrase must be right part of a certain production. However, on the contrary direction, the right part of a production is not necessarily a direct phrase (it can be called direct phrase only when it meet the "if…" conditions). That is to say "right part of a production" is a necessary condition of "direct phrase", but not a sufficient condition. So, in bottom-up analysis process, it is not always the case to perform the reduction operation when meeting the right part of a production. The right part can be reduced only when it meets certain conditions and is assuredly a direct phrase. In order to illustrate in what circumstances an incorrect handle will be incorrectly recognized, we again introduce a natural language example to help students understand it.

For example, if we have the following Chinese grammar:

1. noun phrase $\rightarrow$ noun phrase + noun phrase
2. noun phrase $\rightarrow$ "大" + "会"

Fig. 5 Parse tree of the sentence "乒乓球拍卖大会"

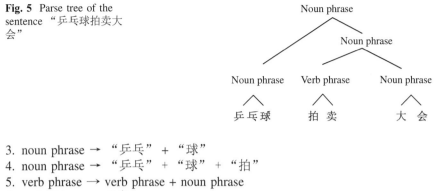

3. noun phrase → "乒乓" + "球"
4. noun phrase → "乒乓" + "球" + "拍"
5. verb phrase → verb phrase + noun phrase
6. verb phrase → "卖"
7. verb phrase → "拍" + "卖"

For the sentence "乒乓球拍卖大会", according to the parse tree shown in Fig. 5, "乒乓球" and "拍卖" is its direct phrase. However, "乒乓球拍" and "卖" are not the sentence's directly phrases although they respectively are right part of productions (4) and (6). But In some other sentences they may be directly phrases, such as in the sentence "商店里的乒乓球拍卖完了". This is why the definition of direct phrase emphasizes that direct phrase is relative to a specific sentence pattern.

4 Conclusions

"Compiler principles" is commonly regarded as the most difficult specialized course in software engineering major because of its difficult theory and abstract content. This chapter attempts to introduce natural language examples into the course. Two examples shown in this chapter demonstrate that this method can liberate students from the abstract theory explanation.

References

1. Li, D., & Shi, H. (2008). Study and exploration of the teaching methods for course "Compiler Principle". *Computer Education, 8*, 103–104.
2. Fillmore, C. J. (1969). Towards a modern theory of case. In D. Reibel & S. Shane (Eds.), *Modern studies in English* (pp. 361–375). Englewood Cliffs, N.J.: Prentice Hall.
3. Fillmore, C. J. (1968). The case for case. In E. Bach & R. Harms (Eds.), *Universals in linguistic theory*. New York: Holt, Rinehart and Winston.

How to Introduce SCRUM into Software Engineering Course

Shaomin Zhu

Abstract In recent years, the Agile methodology as a relatively new approach to software engineering is becoming more popular in industry; and Scrum is the most representative one in the agile practice frameworks or models and is being adopted by more and more IT companies. It is necessary to introduce Scrum into the Software Engineering undergraduate course in our universities to meet the talent requirements from industry. But there are a lot of conflicts between the agile methodology and the traditional software engineering methodology; it will bring some big challenges to us when we introduce Scrum into the software engineering course. In the chapter, the author will explain how to overcome the obstacles in introducing Scrum to Software Engineering based on the past 2-year teaching experience. The results show that the course knowledge system was rebuilt and the better teaching environment was set up successfully. Moreover the students get deeper understanding in software engineering principals and have more interesting in practices of this course.

Keywords Software engineering · Education · Course · Scrum · Agile · Methodology

1 Background

We are entering an era of web-based Internet application and mobile app, and the development mode is changing to meet the new requirements. Because requirements of internet applications or mobile apps are often unclear or unstable, we have to increase iterations to reduce the time to meet the needs of users, and lower

S. Zhu (✉)
School of Software Engineering, Tongji University, Shanghai, China
e-mail: kerryzhu@tongji.edu.cn

G. Motta and B. Wu (eds.), *Software Engineering Education for a Global E-Service Economy*, Progress in IS, DOI: 10.1007/978-3-319-04217-6_3,
© Springer International Publishing Switzerland 2014

the efforts to cope with requirements changes. The Agile methodology is an approach that quickly and inexpensively brings to market complex projects with ill-defined requirements; Agile was born to fill the contemporary situation as a quick-iteration (for example, 2–4 weeks as a development iteration cycle in Scrum, showed in Fig. 1) of software development framework; therefore it is more popular in the recent years, even if it has been existed for 20 years. Of course, software development technology, continuous integration environment, and test automation tools are helping the agile to be a viable approach.

Kent Beck and other 16 prominent members of Agile Alliance published in 2001 the Manifesto for Agile Software Development [1]. They claim they found better ways of developing software from their practices; they also redefined the major activities in software development, i.e.

1. Individuals and interactions over processes and tools.
2. Working software over comprehensive documentation.
3. Customer collaboration over contract negotiation.
4. Responding to change over following a plan.

These values are common to all main agile methods such as Scrum, Extreme Programming, Feature Driven Development, Dynamic Systems Development and so on.

From the Agile Manifesto, it is evident the Agile methodology is a quick iteration approach which focuses on the software product itself and tries to reduce efforts in documentation. Agile caters for new requirements in developing internet applications because requirements always changing during development. Also, Agile puts efforts on the improvement of individual ability, an don team and customer collaboration. In short, it radically different from the traditional methodologies of software engineering.

The traditional methodologies got many foundation ideas from Civil, Construction, or Mechanical Engineering. Actually they can economically and efficiently produce high quality products or projects in front of stable and well-defined requirements. The traditional methodologies represent the amalgamation of management thought in the last century and use scientific management principles that are typical to the efficient mass production. Traditional methodologies emphasize Engineering concept, which focuses on rigid processes, highly structured project plans, comprehensive documentation and other management activities (for example, Change Control Board). The process, planning, standards, normative document templates and project managements are the typical key contents in software engineering (SE) courses. If we do not lecture them in SE courses, what should we address in a SE course? Should we shake the base of SE courses?

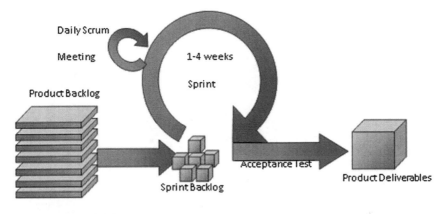

Fig. 1 Scrum model chart

2 How to Make the Students Understand Agile Well

Since SE grew up after many software crises, teachers lecture on SE starting from crises and introducing the rigid normative development process and scientific management [2, 3]. Because application systems have significantly increased in size and complexity, schedule and cost could not be controlled without a system analysis and management discipline. A systematic engineering approach is needed to analyze and solve problems in software development. It is natural to introduce traditional engineering, and it is not difficult to make students understand Waterfall model, V model and Rational Unified process (RUP) [4, 5]. Within the traditional quality management perspective, quality is built in the development cycle, and qualified products are produced by a qualified process. We should control the process starting from customer requirements, and a design can be correct only if you get correct requirements, and, finally a correct coding needs the correct design. Such a process is what a waterfall model implies.

Is Agile, which states that Individuals and interactions over processes and tools, denying the foundations of software engineering? In order to answer the question, we need to review the Agile manifesto "That is, while there is value in the items on the right, we value the items on the left more" and let the students understand the value of processes and tools in the software development. Then we go back to the basic ideas in Agile, whatever we are working for in software development, the requirement definition, design or coding are done by people, i.e. individuals and teams. Nothing can be done in teamwork without collaboration.

Beyond the above conversation [6], we need to build a few models for addressing some puzzles. For example, Agile insists on early and continuous delivery that can bring more value to customers. The model in Fig. 2 can help us to understand it. The features can be used by customers and they bring value to customers as long as the features are released with software products. The shadow

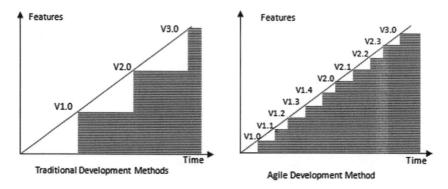

Fig. 2 Values of deliverables comparing traditional method with agile method

area of each chart just shows the value of software deliverables, and the obvious results show that the customers can get much more values from the agile method than the traditional methods.

3 Reconstruction of SE Knowledge

In a traditional SE course, the knowledge system follows Software Engineering Book of Knowledge (SEBOK) [7] and Software Engineering Education (SEEDS) [8], the knowledge system in SE course covers the software development cycle and focuses on the process like CMMI [9], requirement engineering, object-oriented design (OOD), system test and project management. We have to reconstruct the knowledge system for SE course when we introduce the agile method—Scrum into SE course. For instance, we study the typical definition of SE course with 64 class hours, i.e. 4 class hours per week during total 16 weeks. The contents in new syllabus of SE course are listed in Table 1 after enough survey, discussion and reconstruction.

4 Practices on Agile

In a traditional SE course, practice or experimentation is arranged during class teaching. It is easy to make arrangement in the traditional SE course, because of the synchronization between the theory teaching in classroom and the practices in lab. The practice starts from planning a project and goes through requirement analysis and definition, design, coding and testing after the corresponding contents are taught in the classroom. But it is difficult to keep synchronization between

Table 1 The contents and schedule in SE course syllabus

Traditional SE course syllabus	Class hours	New syllabus with Agile after reconstruction of SE course	Class hours
1. Introduction	4	1. Introduction	2
2. Software development cycle	6	2. Traditional methodologies	6
3 Requirement engineering	6	3. Agile method and scrum	4
4. Modeling and UML	8	4. Release planning and spring planning	4
5. Architecture design	4	5. User story (description, priority and estimation)	4
6. Design patterns or user interface (UI) design	6	6. Product backlog and Sprint backlog	4
7. Object-oriented design	8	7. Task execution and daily meetings	4
8. Coding and unit test	5	8. Design (architecture, UI)	6
9. System test	6	9. TDD and Coding	4
10. Maintenance	2	10. Unit test	4
11. Project management	6	11. Continuous integration (including auto deployment and Integration test)	6
12. Review	2	12. Acceptance test	4
13. Exam	3	13. Review meeting and retrospective meeting	2
		14. Continuous delivery	5
		15. Review	2
		16. Exam	3
	64		64

theory and practices in lab, because the iteration is frequent and the period of one sprint is short, and also because its content cannot be completed in the same time.

We clarify the overall framework and key points in Scrum before the students start to do practice. For example, teachers explain the agile Manifesto and the 12 principles underlying the manifesto; then they go through the whole process of Scrum. We allocate more space for students: they raise in the classroom the issues they encounter. This open interaction helps the students better understand Agile methodology or Scrum practices.

However, the above experimentation is not enough. The teachers still help the students to solve the problems on time, which means that a system for the students' practice should be set up so that the teachers can easily track the on-going progress of the given project. The author had 2-year experience in building experimentation environment for SE course practice, so the open source project management system—Redmine [10] is recommended. There is a Scrum plug-in (Scrumbler [10]) in Redmine and students can use it to manage the project in an Agile development. The real case is shown in Fig. 3. This practice will let the students get all necessary development experience from a brand new system (Sprint 1) to a legacy system (Sprint 2, 3 or later).

Students are grouped in small teams. One student in each team plays the role of ScrumMaster and another one plays the role of Product Owner; but they are not qualified. The teacher may play two roles: ScrumMaster of ScrumMaster and

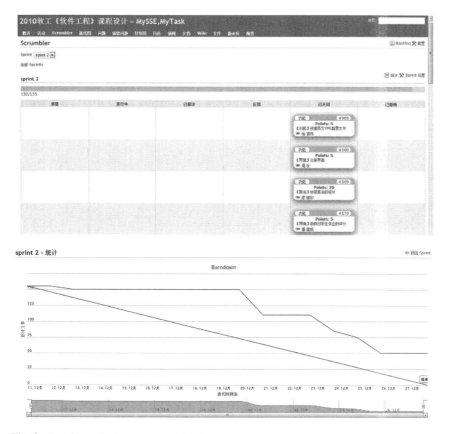

Fig. 3 A real case in SE course with SCRUM

Product Manager, and provide the timely and hands-on instructions to the ScrumMasters and the Product Owners in each student team. This is a key element to make success in the effective practices.

5 Conclusions

We have presented the introduction of Agile methodology in SE course, in order to meet the new requirements. Thoughts, contents and practices of SE course have been discussed, and executed in last 2 years. Results show that the solution is valid and may be regarded as a good reference when other teachers want to introduce the agile methodology into the SE course.

Teaching Scrum software development is a big challenge and requires that the teachers shall have more conversation and collaboration with students. It is better for the students to have good experience in industry. Moreover, the teachers provide more hands-on instructions to students just like coaches, ScrumMaster or Product Manager.

Traditional software engineering is a base, the teachers may introduce classical books such as Tom DeMarco's Peopleware [11], Fred Brooks' The Mythical Man-Month [12] and Watts Humphery's Managing Software Process [2] and so on, and then students can build a solid understanding on software engineering, not limited to Agile aspect. Teachers may make students understand that they work in professional contexts and contexts always are very different because of the wide variety of business, product types and teams. In some cases, traditional methods may be more effective while in other cases, result just is reverse.

References

1. http://www.agilemanifesto.org/
2. Humphery, W. (1989). *Managing software process*. Indianapolis, IN: Addison-Wesley Professional.
3. Naderuzzaman, M., Rabbi, F., & Beg, A. H. (2011). An improved & adaptive software development methodology. *Computer Engineering and Intelligent Systems*, 2(3), USA.
4. Mujumdar, A., Masiwal, G., & Chawan, P. M. (2012). Analysis of various software process models. *International Journal of Engineering Research and Applications (IJERA)*, 2(3), 2015–2021.
5. Osorio, J. A. (2011). Moving from waterfall to iterative development: An empirical evaluation of advantages, disadvantages and risks of RUP. In *37th EUROMICRO Conference on Software Engineering and Advanced Applications* (pp. 453–460), Netherlands.
6. Kessler, R., & Dykman, N. (2007). Integrating traditional and agile processes in the classroom. In *Proceedings of the 38th ACM Technical Symposium on Computer Science Education (SIGCSE 2007)* (pp. 312–316), Covington, Kentucky, USA.
7. Abran, A., Moore, J. W., Bourque, P., & Dupuis, R. (2004). *Guide to the software engineering body of knowledge*. Los Alamitos, CA: IEEE Computer Society.
8. Varma, V. (2005). Case studies: the potential teaching instruments for software engineering education. In *Proceedings of the Fifth International Conference on Quality Software (QSIC 2005)* (pp. 279–284), India.
9. Schneider, K. (2009). *Experience and knowledge management in software engineering*. Berlin, Heidelberg, Germany: Springer.
10. http://www.redmine.org/
11. De Marco, T., & Lister, T. (1999). *Peopleware: Productive projects and teams*. New York, NY: Dorset House Publishing.
12. Brooks, F. (1995). *The mythical man-month: Essays on software engineering, anniversary edition* (2nd ed.). Indianapolis, IN: Addison-Wesley Professional.

Computational Thinking and Its Impact on Software Engineering Education

Dechen Zhan, Lanshun Nie and Xiaofei Xu

Abstract The very rapid development of computers discipline and software discipline has changed various fields of society and nature. Meanwhile, they also extend knowledge space constantly. Hence, the question how to cultivate students has become a key issue for all the educational researchers in computer, software and related disciplines. Currently, more and more people pay attention to a new concept "computational thinking" and study what it brings to computer and software education. Firstly, this article briefly describes computational thinking. Then, we propose a multi-dimensional observation framework of computational thinking-computation tree. Finally, we explore its impact on software engineering education.

Keywords Computational thinking · Service engineering · Software engineering · Education

1 Computation Thinking

In 2006, Prof. Jeannette M. Wing [1] of CMU explicitly proposed concept "Computational Thinking (CT)" and highlighted its universal importance. "Computational thinking involves solving problems, designing systems, and understanding human behavior, by drawing on the concepts fundamental to computer science. Computational thinking includes a range of mental tools that

D. Zhan (✉) · L. Nie · X. Xu
School of Computer Science and Technology, Harbin Institute of Technology,
Harbin, China
e-mail: dechen@hit.edu.cn

L. Nie
e-mail: nls@hit.edu.cn

X. Xu
e-mail: xiaofei@hit.edu.cn

G. Motta and B. Wu (eds.), *Software Engineering Education for a Global E-Service Economy*, Progress in IS, DOI: 10.1007/978-3-319-04217-6_4,
© Springer International Publishing Switzerland 2014

reflect the breadth of the field of computer science." "It represents a universally applicable attitude and skill set everyone, not just computer scientists, would be eager to learn and use." "Thinking like a computer scientist means more than being able to program a computer. It requires thinking at multiple levels of abstraction." It will boost innovation by the cooperation between computing technology and theory/technology of various disciplines, if everyone thinks like computer scientists.

A lot of people consider computational thinking as the third thinking besides "theoretical thinking" and "experimental thinking". Theoretical thinking is characterized by reasoning and deduction. It studies social/natural phenomena and their laws by theoretical means such as assumption/prediction, reasoning and proof. Experimental thinking is characterized by observation and induction. It studies social/natural phenomena and their laws by experiment, observation, and induction. CT is featured by design and construction. It is a kind of "constructive thinking. It studies social/natural phenomena and their laws by computation means. As we are required to explore society/nature more deeply and extensively, traditional methods including theoretical and experimental means are not effective enough. For example, it is difficult to get sound result from massive experimental data merely by observation or induction. Then, it is inevitable to use computation thinking and tools to address this problem.

How to summarize the important CTs embodied in computing disciplines? This paper presents a new model which is entitled "computation tree" for observing computational thinking.

2 Computation Tree

What "core" CTs there exists in computing (computer) discipline? What impacts CT will bring on students and deeply change students' thinking? Exploration and answer to this question are helpful to the cultivation, curriculum design and course design of computer/software disciplines.

Since the invention of computer in 1940s, development of computing technology and systems is like a leafy tree which grows and develops continuously. Based on this fact, we draw the development into a tree, as shown in Fig. 1. We call it "Computation Tree".

2.1 Root-Groundbreaking Thinking of Computing Technology and System

The root reflects the core, most basic, or groundbreaking technologies or ideas of computing technology and system. Until today or even in the future, these ideas

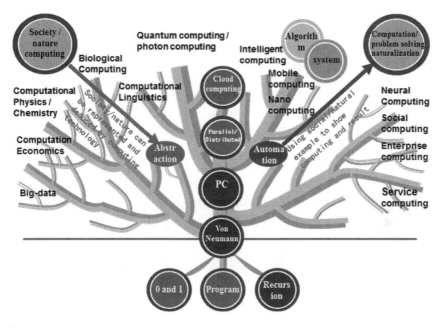

Fig. 1 Computation tree

still play a significant role in the study of new computing means. Based on a careful analysis of these ideas, this chapter argues that "0 and 1", "program" and "recursion" are the three most important thinking.

- "0 and 1" thinking: "0 and 1" thinking reflects five basic thinking, i.e. semantic can be represented symbolically, symbol can be computed, all the computation can be encoded into 0 and 1, 0 and 1 can be implemented by hardware automatically, system can be constructed hierarchically and compositionally, components and systems can be fabricated into IC. It also reflects the basic link between software and hardware, and the most underlying abstraction and automation. So it is one of the most important kinds of computational thinking.
- "Program" thinking: How to implement a complex system? A system is composed by both basic operations (they are easy to implement) and compositional operations (volatile, complex operations can be implemented by various compositions of basic operations). Therefore to implement a system is equal to implementing basic operations plus implementing a controller which controls the composition of basic operations and its execution order. Instruction is used to control basic operation. Program is the various combinations of instructions and its execution order. The system can perform complex functions by control the execution of "instruction" in accordance with "program". Computer or computing system are those machines and systems which have the ability to perform a variety of program. So, "instructions and program" thinking is another most kind of computational thinking.

- "Recursion" thinking: Recursion is a typical feature of computing technology. It can be used to implement a program which performs nearly infinitely functionality with only finite number of steps. Recursion technology includes recursive process, recursive algorithm, recursive procedures. Recursive procedure is a procedure which calls itself. Recursive algorithm is an algorithm including a recursive process. Recursive program is a program which calls itself directly or indirectly. Complex problems can be represented and solved by recursively calling itself or high-end calling low-end. Hence, "recursion" thinking is another most important kind of computation thinking.

2.2 Trunk: Evolutionary Thinking of General-Purpose Computing Environment

The trunk reflects the development and evolution of general-purpose computing environment, i.e. computing systems. In-depth understanding of computational thinking reflected by general-purpose computing systems means great significance for the understanding and applying computational methods to the study in various disciplines. It is especially important to the study of specialized computing methods.

- Von Neumann machine: Von Neumann computer embodied the basic thinking of the stored-procedure and automatic execution of procedure. Program and data are stored beforehand in the memory. Instructions are fetched and analyzed by a controller from memory step by step. Instructions are translated into various electrical signals according to clock pulse. It reflects how program is stored and is executed by CPU (controller and operator). Understanding Von Neumann architecture has important implications for algorithm and program design.
- Personal computing environment: Personal computer mostly follows Von Neumann architecture. Storage resources are extended and a storage architecture is constituted by registers, memory (RAM/ROM), external memory (hard disk/ CD-ROM/floppy disk). Program is stored in persistent memory (external memory). It is loaded into memory and then executed by the CPU runtime. Operating system is introduced to manage computing resources. It embodies the basic thinking of how program in the storage architecture is executed on hardware under the assistance of OS.
- Parallel and distributed computing environments: Parallel distributed computing environments are usually complex server environment composed by multiple CPUs, multiple disk arrays and have strong parallel distributed processing capabilities. This environment is usually applied to build computing system in local area network/wide area network. It embodies the basic thinking of how program is executed parallel and distributed by hardware in networked environment (multi-core, multi-disk arrays) under the assistance of OS.

- Cloud computing environment: Cloud computing environment is usually composed by high-performance computing nodes (multi-CPU) and high-capacity disk storage nodes. To take full advantage of the computing and storage nodes, "virtual machine" and/or "virtual disks" are dynamically configured on-demand. Each virtual machine performs programs like a physical computer. A virtual disk stores data like a physical disk. It embodies the basic thinking of resource virtualization and service-oriented resource provision on-demand.

2.3 Two-Color Branches: Alternatively Promote and Co-Evolution of Problem Solving Thinking

Problem-solving thinking, which means solving problems in society and nature by computing, mainly consists of two aspects: algorithms and systems. They are alternatively promoted and co-evolve.

- "Algorithm": Algorithm is known as the soul of computing. An algorithm is a set of finite rules. It defines the sequence of operations to solve a particular kind of problems. Or it provides a series of steps for task execution or problem solving. Design algorithm is the key to solve a problem. The algorithm should be implementable, finish in finite time and utilize finite memory space and be as fast as possible.
- "System": Although algorithm is the soul of computing, we also need system. System is the bridge and integration between computation and society/natural environment. Systems provide ubiquitous, transparent, optimized and comprehensive solutions to society and nature problem. A system is composed of interrelated elements which interacts each other. It has a specific structure and functions as a whole. Design and development of computing systems (such as hardware systems, software systems, network systems, information systems, applications, etc.) is a complex and challengeable work. How to control the complexity of a system? How to model a complex system consistently using various modeling technology? How to optimize system structure in order to guarantee the reliability, security, etc.? All these can not be solved without "system" thinking or "system science" thinking.

2.4 Small Branches: Fusion Thinking Between Computing and Social/Natural Environment

Small branches reflect various research directions of computing discipline, such as intelligent computing, pervasive computing, personal computing, social computing, enterprise computing, service computing. It also reflects new research directions from the interaction of computing discipline and other disciplines, such as computational physics, computational chemistry, computational biology, computational linguistics, computational economics.

- "Society/nature computing": The link from branches to trunks reflects society/nature computing, i.e. social/natural phenomena can be represented and deduced by computing technology. It emphasizes on the use of computational methods to deduce/discover social/natural laws.
- "Computation/problem solving naturalization": The link from trunk to branches reflects computation/problem solving naturalization. It emphasizes on the use of social/natural example to show the process and result of computing and problem solving.

They essentially reflect basic thinking of "computing systems at different levels of abstraction". The core of them is "abstraction" and "automation". Simply, it can be divided into three levels.

- Machine level—Protocol (abstraction) and encoder/decoder/converter (automation) are used to solve the interaction between machine and machine;
- Man–machine level—Language (abstraction) and compiler/actuators (automation) are used to solve the interaction between man and machine;
- Business level—Model (abstraction) and execution engine/execution systems (automation) are used to solve the interaction between business systems and computing systems.

The fusion between computing and social/natural environment promotes the formation of networked society. LAN/WAN, Internet, WWW, Internet of Things, Internet of Service, Social Network promote the interconnection of among physical objects and people. Networked environment and networked society greatly changed people's thinking, and the way of living, working, traveling, etc.

3 Impact on SE Education

Software engineering discipline grows with the development of computer discipline. It focuses on studying and applying engineering methods to build and maintain effective, practical and high-quality "software". Software engineering disciplines can also be discussed under framework "computation tree", as shown in Fig. 2. Three concentric semi-circles are drawn from trunk to branches. Then we can analyze the emergence and development of software engineering discipline, and how it is impacted by computational thinking.

- "Software" layer: "software" is located in inner circle. It develops with the development of computing methods, i.e. from Von Neumann computer to personal computing environment and parallel distributed computing environments. System software developed gradually and became mature. Applications software grew and expands continuously to all fields.

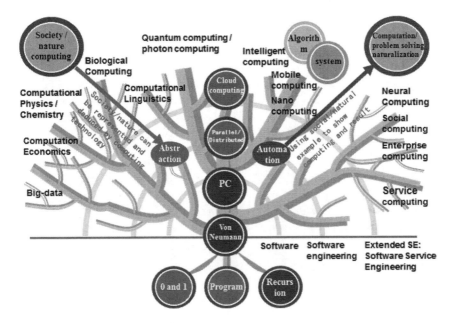

Fig. 2 SE from the perspective of computation tree

- "Software engineering" layer: "software engineering" is located in middle circular layer. With the development of parallel/distributed environment and the mature of computer/network technology, software becomes large-scale "system". Questions such as how to ensure correctness of "system", how to develop and maintain "system" in low-cost gradually become the focus of research. Then, software engineering disciplines appears and forms.
- "Extended software engineering–software service engineering" layer: Software service engineering is located in outer layer. Computing means has evolved from parallel/distributed environment to cloud computing environment. Computing technology is now deeply integrated with society and nature. Network has evolved from machine network, information network to Internet of Things, Social Network, and Internet of Service. Thus, more attention is paid to "software service". Software engineering discipline also extends to software service engineering.

3.1 Software Morphology and Characteristics Change Under New Environment

Traditional software engineering concerns software characteristics such as modifiability, efficiency, reliability, understandability, maintainability, reusability, adaptability, portability, traceability, and interoperability. It emphasizes studying technology and theory for implementing software with these features.

Software morphology changes in new environment (parallel distributed environment, cloud computing environment, deep integration of computation and social/natural environment). The most important change is the extension from "software" to "service". Nowadays, people concern more about the usage of software, pay-per-use, anytime, anywhere. Infrastructure, platform, software, and everything become service and are delivered as a service (IaaS, PaaS, SaaS, EaaS). This changes not only the way of software delivery, but also the ways of software usage, development and maintenance. A lot of new features are added to and essential to "software" due to these changes. Technology and theory about how to implement software with these features are hot research topics of software service engineering discipline. These new features include but not limited to: mass users, user-oriented scalability, systems-oriented large-scale resource scheduling, uninterrupted service, self-evolution, multi-tenant, distributed, parallel, large-scale heterogeneous data virtualization, interoperability and synergy.

3.2 From SE to Extended SE

Traditional software engineering concerns software life cycle and studies on methods, theories and tools in various stages of life cycle (such as software requirements, software design, software implementation, software testing, software maintenance). It concerns software architecture and software development methods under its guide. It also concerns software process, software project management, software configuration management, and software quality management.

To address the changes of software morphology and characteristics under new environment, software services engineering which is an extension of traditional SE concerns more about:

- Software service ecosystem—Internet provides an online delivery and evolution environment. It also is an ecosystem in which software producers, software operators, and software users participate and interact.
- Theory and technology of software process blending—All activities such as software requirements, design, implementation, testing, operation, and evolution interact in unique ecosystem. Also, various processes blend in a single environment.
- New features of software service—It includes the above mentioned new features of software services and techniques/theory described to implement them. It also includes development methodology of software service in new environment and meeting new requirement.
- Everything as a service—EaaS/BPaaS, SaaS, PaaS, IaaS, and hierarchical computing resource as a service.

3.3 Software Engineering Discipline Education

Based on the analysis under computation tree framework, software engineering discipline is deeply influenced and shaped by computational thinking. Thus, education of software engineering discipline should adapt to these changes.

1. **Emphasizing CT education and division/combination among liberal thinking education, skills training and knowledge expansion in software engineering discipline**

   Firstly, thinking inspires people to imagine and to be innovative. Thinking is not only conceptual, but also figurative. It is also universal. Although knowledge and skill may decrease in terms of time, thinking does not. Knowledge and skills may even be forgotten, but thinking may be subtle and integrated into further innovation activities. Therefore, liberal thinking education should be emphasized in SE education. Thinking such as "0 and 1", "program" can help students form thinking mode of study and applying abstraction and automation to solve problem. Thinking such as "parallel distributed computing", "cloud computing" can help students form new thinking mode of merging physical space/virtual space and applying parallel computing, distributed computing, virtual computing to solve social/natural problems. Thinking such as "algorithm" and "system" help students form thinking mode of converting complex into simple, and applying methods such as OO to solve problem. SaaS, EaaS are evidences that software engineering is influenced and changed by computational thinking. With deeper fusion between computing technology and society/nature, thinking is more and more important to innovation. When strengthening liberal thinking education, we should also pay attention to various essential education levels, i.e. suitable division and combination of liberal thinking education, skills training and knowledge expansion. It is not enough to just educate thinking. We should also teach essential knowledge and provide continuous, sufficient training to students. In doing so, thinking will become students' capability. So, three level courses should be planned in curriculum for computational thinking, skills training, and knowledge expansion, respectively. Then, we can optimize knowledge structure and strengthen capability of software engineering discipline talent.

2. **Necessary to extend teaching from traditional SE to software service engineering**

   Based on the above analysis, changes in the computing environment and formation of network society have all contributed to the expansion from SE to software service engineering. Therefore, traditional SE teaching should also be extended to software service engineering teaching. Traditional SE education is usually based on knowledge structure organized according to software life cycle. It strengthen teaching knowledge and skills in "software requirements", "software design", "software construction", "software testing" and "software

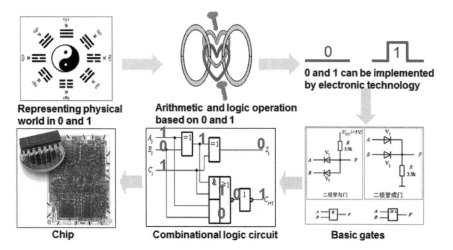

Fig. 3 Systematic computational thinking and presenting it in a visual and implementable way

maintenance". It also strengthen teaching management knowledge and skills in "software process", "software project", "software configuration", "software quality", etc. Software service engineering teaching should be further extended on the basis of traditional SE teaching. In liberal thinking education level, teaching service-oriented computing thinking should be strengthened. In skill training level, teaching and training service modeling, SaaS software development technology, SOA & ESB, cloud computing and cloud services, workflow should be strengthened. In knowledge expansion level, knowledge in service engineering methodology, service business optimization and scheduling, distributed and concurrency, system optimization and evolution, Big data processing, domain service engineering, service performance optimization, services security, and service management technology should be taught.

3. **Emphasizing systematic thinking education, case driven teaching, and visual teaching**

Thinking is a complete solution which is composed of a series of knowledge. Each step of thinking may need knowledge to pave the way and can be understood based on some knowledge. The whole solution can be entirely understood by systematically understanding and integrating all the steps. This systematic thinking is "implementable thinking rather than the details of implementation". So it should be taught visually and in an implementable way. For example, "0 and 1" thinking can be taught visually as in Fig. 3. "Knowledge" is introduced step by step when teaching "thinking". "Thinking" forms systematically when "knowledge" is ready and connected. Capacity increases when thinking is understood.

When teaching service-oriented computing thinking, particular the mapping between "service business" and "software", case based teaching is an

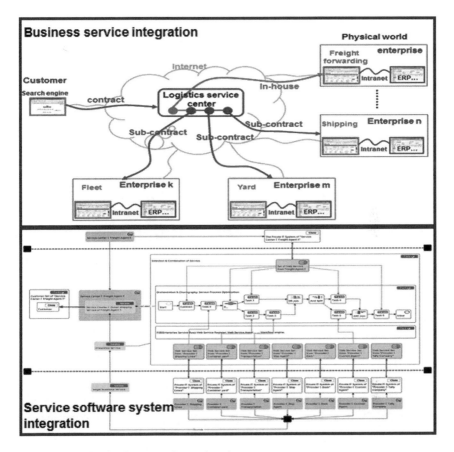

Fig. 4 Case study of software service engineering

important means. When explaining service composition, logistics service integration inside/across enterprise is a good case. Business integration covers enterprise level, business process level and resource level. Software covers the integration of business components, Web Services, workflows and service business. All this is shown in Fig. 4. Software engineering service tools are necessary means for case based teaching. Tools will support students to explore problem solving. If there is enough large-scale cases which covers whole process of some domain, an experiential teaching based on these cases is important and perfect to cultivate service-orient computational thinking.

4. **Necessary to study software service engineering knowledge system in-depth in order to guide teaching practice**

SWEBOK [2], i.e. Software Engineering Body of Knowledge, which is famous in SE discipline, is widely adopted by and used as a guideline to teaching practices in universities. With the trend of software engineering servitization, software service engineering will plays more and more important role in software engineering discipline. Typical examples are service-oriented software engineering, software-enabled service engineering, software plus service plus engineering. Software service engineering covers both economic-oriented business service and IT-oriented Web Service or software service. How to map business service to IT/software service constitutes basic contents of software service engineering. Knowledge system of software service engineering should be established by learning and referring to SWEBOK. If an effective software engineering knowledge system is well established, it is important and helpful to the education development of software engineering discipline.

4 Conclusions

Computational thinking includes a lot, such as groundbreaking thinking of computing technology and system, evolutionary thinking of general-purpose computing environment, alternatively promote and co-evolution of problem solving thinking, fusion thinking between computing and social/natural environment, etc.

By carefully observing SE under the framework of computational thinking, SE develops into software service engineering in new computing environment. Software service engineering has its unique research area. Software services engineering concerns more about software ecosystem.

Education in SE discipline should be extended to cover software service engineering. It should be extended in different levels such as computational thinking, skill training, and knowledge expansion.

Courses, curriculum, knowledge architecture should be well designed for software service engineering education. It is an ongoing problem worth to be research.

References

1. Wing, J. M. (2006). Computational thinking. *Communications of the ACM, 49*(3), 33.
2. SWEBOK, http://www.computer.org/portal/web/swebok.

Electronic Online Marking of Software Assignments

Gary Hill and Scott Turner

Abstract With the advent of Virtual Learning Environments (VLEs) and online electronic submission of assignments, computing lecturers are increasingly assessing code online. There are various tools for aiding electronic marking, grading and plagiarism detection. However, there appears to be limited shared advice to computer science tutors (and students) on the effective use of these tools. This chapter aims to stimulate peer-discussion amongst tutors involved in the assessing (marking and grading) of software code. Many United Kingdom (UK) Higher Education Institutions (HEI) are using electronic marking. This chapter discusses the authors' experience and proposes suggestions for appropriate and effective solutions to the electronic assessment of software code. This will be based on the authors' experience of electronically assessing code over three academic years and the current advice given to their students.

Keywords Software engineering · Online marking · Online grading · Online assessment · Turnitin · Computer code

1 Introduction

Traditionally computer sciences courses will assess software code at various stages throughout a student's education. The authors have previously [1] discussed issues surrounding a formal code referencing method that would assist in good practice

G. Hill (✉) · S. Turner
Department of Computing and Immersive Technologies, University of Northampton,
Northampton, UK
e-mail: Gary.Hill@northampton.ac.uk

S. Turner
e-mail: Scott.Turner@northampton.ac.uk

G. Motta and B. Wu (eds.), *Software Engineering Education for a Global
E-Service Economy*, Progress in IS, DOI: 10.1007/978-3-319-04217-6_5,
© Springer International Publishing Switzerland 2014

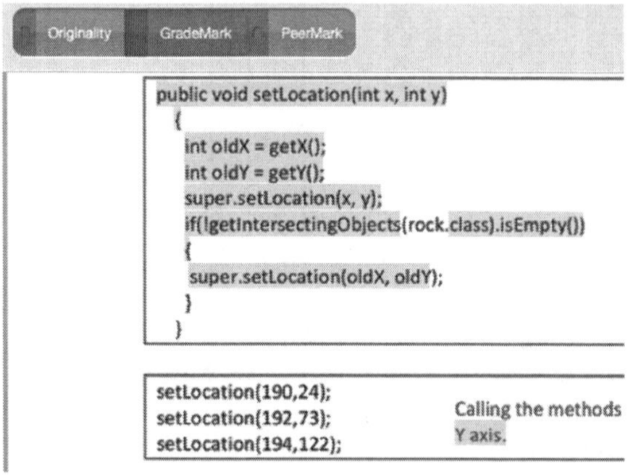

Fig. 1 Similarity

and plagiarism prevention. The issue introduced here is how to deal with electronic online marking of software assignments that are an essential assessed element of any Computer Science course.

1.1 Background of EOMOSA/SAGE

The University of Northampton introduced a limited pilot (Academic Year (AY) 2010/2011) called SAGE (Submission and Grading Electronically) for the electronic online **submission** and **marking** of assignments. SAGE was extended to the whole University (AY2011/2012) and is currently in its third years of operation (AY2012/2013). The Department of Computing and Immersive Technologies volunteered to pilot SAGE in a number of their year one (Level 4) undergraduate modules. One of these (CSY1020 Problem Solving and Programming) required the submission of computer code.

1.2 Tools Used for EOMOSA

The SAGE pilot used a VLE (Blackboard) for the module notes, with assignment submission using turnitin [2] as the plagiarism detection software. To conduct the marking a GradeMark [3] plugin tool is used alongside turnitin to allow simultaneous viewing of two overlays/layers showing the originality of the assignment usually highlighted (Figs. 1 and 2) and the markers comments. Within Grademark, there is an option to add generic or commonly used comments/advice as well as individual unique comments [4].

Fig. 2 Highlighting possible matches

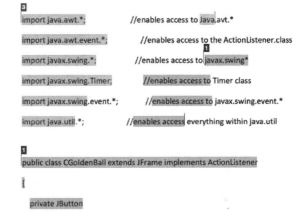

2 Code Submission

The first constraint was that the SAGE project assumed there would be a single file submission. Initially this did not seem to be an issue, as code submission/listings were traditionally appended to a technical report. Tutors would then mark the report and code together. When considering the similarity reports produced by turnitin (plagiarism prevention) for the combined technical report and appended code, it was felt that there would be an expected differential of originality for a technical report compared with the code appendix. At this stage it was felt that two separate electronic submissions would be required (one for the report and the other for the code/appendix). There were other constraints due to document **size restrictions** of 20 MB [5] and the **limited file formats** (.doc, .wpd, .eps, .pdf, .htm, .rtf and .txt) [5] accepted by turnitin. Word documents were chosen, with the code pasted (in colour to include syntax highlighting) from the various Integrated Development Environments (IDEs) that had been used. Additionally advice was given to student on how to keep within the size limit for their submissions—allowing two file submissions helped to alleviate this problem. It should also be noted that ALL code assignments were demonstrated to the marking tutors on a separate assessment day, with a consistent marking sheet used to appropriately assess the working prototype applications produced.

3 Code Originality

The authors have previously discussed [1] and proposed good practice for the appropriate referencing for code. They proposed a code referencing structure for a typical class/source file to be:

- Header
- Disclaimer/copyright
- References
- Code

With a traditional report there is an approximate percentage of similarity that is seen as acceptable, but left to the discretion and interpretation by the module tutor. A tutor can even set up whether to exclude quotes and small percentage matches. The acceptable percentage of originality from the experience gained through the SAGE pilot and implementation was approximately 25 %. Interestingly there appears to be limited consensus on an acceptable similarity percentage, but 25 % (e.g. University of Teeside [6]) depending on the nature of the assignment, does seem to be a common value. Once a report exceeded this percentage a tutor would investigate where the similarity occurred within the report. This could be referenced correctly or most commonly was the reuse of items given in the assignment brief e.g. aim, objectives, functionality/complexity requirements etc.

The expectations for the percentage of similarity for computer code was a difficult value to ascertain. From experience, for assignment tasks predominantly with code listings, it was felt that any similarity report that indicated 70 % commonality or above required investigation and interpretation from the marker. It is recognised that this will vary from assignment to assignment. The reasons for the variation and, perhaps what some may consider, high percentage similarity can be explained. The students were strictly taught Java using an essential text [7] and the entire module notes and exercises were taken from this. The students were only directed to one other web resource, which included the language specification [8] and the associated/official tutorial site [9] maintained by Oracle. Therefore it was expected that there would be reuse of code from the book exercises and the standard constructs, preferred naming conventions emphasised in lectures, and that this would contribute to a higher percentage of originality than usual. In addition, the assignment used a problem-based approach [7], where from their first lecture they had been given the problem and worked towards a solution weekly. Advice was given and group discussion conducted to work through the problem. With the use of a common client brief and a problem based approach, where alongside learning Java for the first time, all new concepts were applied directly to the assignment.

The increasing level of complexity and depth of Java taught was immediately demonstrated and applied to the assignment, which usually manifested itself as increased application functionality or complexity of Graphical User Interface (GUI).

4 Electronic Marking Benefits

Once the marking tutor has ascertained the 'appropriate' percentage of similarity, the tutor needs to undertake the daunting task of the marking. The authors would argue that the benefits to the students and tutor include improved:

Fig. 3 Extract of feedback

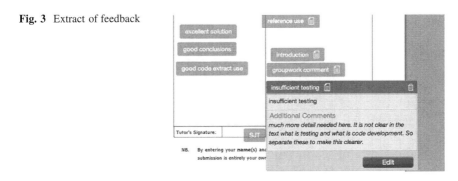

- Feedback quality/consistency
- Submission, access and release
- Transparency
- Turnaround.

4.1 Feedback Quality/Consistency

The opportunity exists within turnitin to use a QuickMark [4] plugin that enables the saving of standardised feedback comments that can be used across all assignments. Once a set of standardised comments have been developed, these can be refined from year to year and the tutor and students find that the feedback becomes more extensive and meaningful. The standard QuickMark [4] comments can be used and then easily edited to personalise the comments (Fig. 3). In the authors' experience, whilst the generic feedback is used, it is enhanced and enriched over time, but also the option to then personalise this feedback is invaluable. In addition, the tutor will also add specific and very focused individual comments.

4.2 Submission, Access and Release

There are the obvious benefits of students being able to remotely submit their assignments and the resulting ease of remote access by the marking tutor. Even the submission times tend to be late evening—normally 23:59! Marking tutors can download the assignment locally or mark online and once marked, students can download an annotated, marked and graded version of their assignment. There is no need for the past complications of students getting access to the hard copy to ensure timely and appropriate feedback. At the University ALL the assignment grades and comments are released and available electronically to the students within 3 weeks after the initial submission. The release dates are consistent across all modules to help with the students expectations of when grades and comments are released.

4.3 Transparency

Access to the work by second markers, moderators and external examiners becomes a simple process of granting full instructor access to the VLE module. This is very helpful in ensuring access can be gained from remote sites, where courses are franchised within Europe or internationally. In addition external examiners can have full access to the marking and moderation processes within the module and can chose at random their chosen sample of work for their consideration. External examiners will need additional training/induction to ensure the ease of access to the modules and assessments to enable effective monitoring and evaluation.

4.4 Turnaround

The automated release date for the assignment marking assists the students and staff to get access to their grades and comments. In addition, by refining and enhancing the feedback/comments, experience has shown that the assignment marking becomes more efficient and effective than previous hard copy submissions. The authors would estimate that the marking time has been reduced by around 25 %. Many of the issues discussed as general comments or examples of good practice comments are not only repeated for different assignments, from academic year to academic year, but also between students work. The time taken in writing these comments again is saved and the option of editing existing comments or writing new individual comments is also used.

In the author's opinion the quality of feedback has also improved, by time being taken on developing the comments that are regularly used or generic, being richer with the use of the option to enhance/edit these comments further for individual cases.

5 Discussion

The purpose of this chapter was to stimulate discussion from peers involved in software engineering education, around their experiences of using Electronic Online Marking of Software Assignments (EOMOSA) and the educational benefits to both the students and the marking tutor. It is hoped that the discussions prompted by this chapter may lead to further benefits and appropriate solutions/consensus on EOMOSA.

6 Conclusions

The authors have attempted to share their experiences of using Electronic Online Marking of Software Assignments (EOMOSA) emphasising some of the issues that need to be considered. The main conclusions are that:

- The code should be submitted in a separate document from any technical report;
- Software assignments should be seen as special cases in terms of the higher originality scores than may be found in other disciplines due to the nature of the assignments:
  - Expected standard constructs and reuse of code;
  - Single problem/client based assignments;
  - Group work, whether formally or informally part of the assessment, which we expected from a computing professional.

- The code similarity report will indicate a high percentage of similarity that will need to be interpreted at the discretion of the marking tutor;
- Generic reusable feedback can be edited to enrich/enhance and personalise to improve the quality of feedback;
- Marking times can be reduced after the initial constructing of the generic feedback;
- Assignment submission and post marking access by the student is more versatile;
- Having the option of including generic reusable feedback does lead to students getting feedback that is not useful.

It is hoped that the above discussions will assist in easing any anxiety felt by module tutors that are faced with the potentially daunting prospect of Electronic Online Marking of Software Assignments (EOMOSA).

References

1. Hill, G., & Turner, S. (2012). Referencing within code in software engineering education! *Computer Education, 10*(166), 1–4. (ISSN: 1672-5913).
2. Turnitin. [online]. (2013). Available from: https://turnitin.com/static/index.php [Accessed 06/02/13].
3. GradeMark [online]. (2013). Available from: http://submit.ac.uk/en_gb/products/grademark [Accessed 06/02/13].
4. QuickMark [online]. (2013). Available from: http://turnitin.com/en_us/support/help-center/creating-quickmark-sets [Accessed 06/02/13].
5. Turner, S., & Hill, G. (2010). Innovative use of robots and graphical programming in software education. *Computer Education, 9*, 54–56. (ISSN: 1672-5913).
6. University of Teeside [online]. (2012). Available from: https://eat.scm.tees.ac.uk/bb8content/resources/recipes/interpretTurnitin.pdf [Accessed on 06/02/13].

7. Douglas Bell, D., & Parr, M. (2010). *Java for students* (6th ed.). NJ: Prentice Hall. 027373122X.
8. Java API Specification [online]. (2013). Available from: http://docs.oracle.com/javase/7/docs/api/ [Accessed 06/02/13].
9. [Java Tutorial [online]. (2013). Available from: http://docs.oracle.com/javase/tutorial/index.html [Accessed 06/02/13].

Learning in the Context of an Ambient Assisted Living Apartment: Including Methods of Serious Gaming

Sven Leonhardt, Stephan Kassel, Anne Randow and Tobias Teich

Abstract Due to demographic change and the resulting challenges for society, innovative solutions are needed to maintain the living quality of the elderly. In the research project Ambient Assisted Living in Intelligent Controlled Environments (A^2LICE) a (technical) system to maintain the self-determination and autonomy of older people in their home environment is developed. By using facility automation and smart homes, the foundations of assisting people in need for help in their own homes are created. But supporting older people with technical assistance systems is bearing challenges beyond the technical issues. Acceptance problems and the lack of willingness to learn in the main target group lead to problems in the implementation of the ideas. To avoid these problems and demonstrate the advantages of Ambient Assisted Living technologies to the users, methods from other research disciplines are integrated. The approach of Serious Gaming is focusing on using the intrinsic motivation of individuals for learning. This should solve fundamental issues of acceptance and knowledge expansion in older generations. By utilizing the effect of playful learning and by connecting familiar concepts with new ones, users of Ambient Assisted Living technologies are getting easier access to these systems and their operations.

Keywords Ambient assisted living · Aging society · Serious gaming · Life-long learning · Intelligent controlled environment

S. Leonhardt (✉) · S. Kassel · A. Randow · T. Teich
Institute for Management and Information, University of Applied Sciences, Zwickau, Germany
e-mail: sven.leonhardt@fh-zwickau.de

S. Kassel
e-mail: Stephan.Kassel@fh-zwickau.de

A. Randow
e-mail: anne.randow@fh-zwickau.de

T. Teich
e-mail: tobias.teich@fh-zwickau.de

G. Motta and B. Wu (eds.), *Software Engineering Education for a Global E-Service Economy*, Progress in IS, DOI: 10.1007/978-3-319-04217-6_6,
© Springer International Publishing Switzerland 2014

Fig. 1 Conceptual gap in the
healthcare process

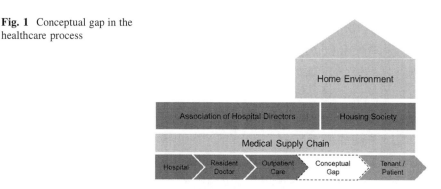

1 Introduction: Research in Ambient Assisted Living

In the research project "Ambient Assisted Living in Intelligent Controlled Environments" (A^2LICE), funded by the European Social Fund (ESF), the integration of Ambient Assisted Living into the context of smart homes is evaluated in an interdisciplinary team consisting of specialists from the faculty for health and nursing science, the faculty for computer science and the faculty for business administration at Zwickau University of Applied Sciences, and the Chair of factory planning at the Technical University of Chemnitz. This research is focusing on a conceptual gap in the public healthcare system (Fig. 1). This gap lies between stationary or outpatient treatment in specialized institutions and the care for patients in their familiar home living environment [1].

The primary objective of this research project, which was started in July 2012, lies in enabling older people to live their own, independent life, for a long time, by providing an apartment with a specific design and technical equipment. The equipment is based on practical, available and affordable technical systems, which are tailored to the individual goals and preferences of the elder people interacting with these systems [1].

The research area of Ambient Assisted Living (AAL) is a relatively young research discipline. AAL includes concepts, products and services to combine new technologies with the social setting and to improve the fitting. This aims in increasing the quality of life for people in all stages of life. Thus AAL could be translated into "Age-compliant assistance systems for a healthy and independent life." This is outlining that AAL is mainly focusing on the individual person in his direct environment [2].

Ambient Assisted Living is considered by many experts as a major contribution to maintaining or improving the quality of care and service for elder people. The increasing proportion of older people in the total population is challenging the society and the health system in a totally new way. Aging in health and maintaining personal autonomy despite of limitations caused by age are therefore relevant political and social goals. An important topic of gerontological nursing research is how this autonomy can be obtained facing the natural reduction of physical or mental fitness [3]. This includes that the elder should live on their own as long as possible despite health restrictions [4].

2 Preserving the Autonomy of Older People in Their Home Environment

To maintain the autonomy of the elderly in their apartment but at the same time improve their safety, ambient sensors are used in their home environment, allowing a monitoring of activities and behavior of the people. The technology for smart homes and building automation is integrated unobtrusively into their familiar house and provides numerous unobtrusive support options. The main interaction facility for the residents with the assisting system is the mobile screen (tablet PC). By providing software which analyzes sensor and vital patient data, a rapid intervention in emergency situations is possible. But also the recording and analysis of (health) data over time creates added value for the participants. Long-term stationary hospital stays can be avoided sometimes, because the progress of diseases can be monitored as well in the peoples' home environment. On top of these monitoring applications, additional solutions can be provided in the field of robotics, where people with physical disabilities are actively supported.

Because of the multi-disciplinary approach of Ambient Assisted Living possibilities for technical assistance seem endless. End users of these technologies are the target group of people older than 65 years. However, numerous studies have shown that especially this target group is not technologically adept [5]. Therefore, an inevitable requirement for these ambient systems lies in a simple and intuitive way to learn the interaction with the systems.

3 Lifelong Learning

At this point we want to reference the principle of *lifelong learning*. This is a concept for enabling people to learn autonomously throughout their life span. It relies on the information independence of the individuals. "You can't teach an old dog new tricks" is no longer valid today. Learning does not stop after school, vocational training or university education. Learning is the essential tool for acquiring knowledge and thus for shaping individual living and working opportunities. Lifelong Learning is the key phrase for competing in the labor market, making up for a professional or educational degree, or simply continuing one's abilities [6]. This widely acknowledged definition of lifelong learning is insufficient, latest with the reference to Ambient Assisted Living. Especially older people, living with the motivation to maintain their independence and autonomy at a great age, are now for the first time enabled by Ambient Assisted Living technologies. But they have to start to learn many basic handling and control concepts. This results in numerous challenges not occurring in "normal" (adult) education. New and innovative methods and approaches to learning and motivating elder people have to be designed. Different studies on Ambient Assisted Living are stating that low or lacking acceptance are the biggest barrier to the widespread adoption and use of these technologies among the potential users. This low acceptance mainly results from fear of the older users to not being able to operate these technical devices. On top, many elderly are lacking the motivation to deal with completely new topics in their final stage of life.

4 Serious Gaming: Methodological Learning in an AAL Environment

These barriers for learning processes are not new. In a growing number of instances, exactly these problems of learning are tackled by a serious gaming approach. Especially in the field of corporate learning, these approaches are currently strongly discussed. Studies from Organizational Science have shown that playful intervention is encouraging learning and critical reflection. Apart from these individual effects serious gaming is also attributed to encourage shared knowledge in groups, and to provide principles for heuristic ways to goal-oriented action in a dynamic environment [7, 8].

Serious Games are defined as mostly digital games providing information, knowledge and skills in an entertaining way. They are not only focusing on fun, but also offering an added value [9]. A differentiation to the terms of game-based learning or learning games is difficult, but two aspects are typically emphasized in Serious Games: (1) They are not designed primarily for educational or business situations, and (2) They interweave the learning part with the game flow, to enable true "playful learning" [10]. This type of learning seems ideally suited for the needs of the Ambient Assisted Living and the associated challenge of learning for older people.

There are numerous application areas for these fundamental learning methods (see Table 1). On the one hand, the older people can easily learn how to operate the systems and get used to an interaction with the computer, which is new for many of them. On the other hand, the games can be directly used for the care and rehabilitation of the users. With such serious games, the intrinsic motivations of the elderly residents to learn independently and to maintain their cognitive abilities can be used. Especially games which are already known by the older people from the analog world (like cards, board games, crosswords, etc.), are suited. With these exercises for logics, math, memory, perception and matching skills, the players can train their minds. This is appreciated by older people. They are looking forward to cognitive challenges and love to puzzle. Many elderly people have the desire to train the skills that are important in the real world now or have been important in

Table 1 Classification scheme for serious games [12]

Taxonomy	Games of health	Adver-games	Training games	Education games	Science games	Production	Games at work
Politics and NGO	Public health education	Awareness and political information	Worker education	Public interest and awareness	Data acquisition and planning	Strategic and political planning	Public opinion polls and diplomacy
Defense	Rehabilitation and wellness	Recruiting and propaganda	Training and education	Continuing education measures	Strategy and planning	Defense research and preparation for conflicts	Control mechanics and operations control
Health-care	Cyber therapy (exergaming)	Wellness campaign/prevention	Training games/ professional education	Patient education/illness management	Visualization and epidemic research	Biotech design and production	Public healthcare
Marketing and Communication	Advertising and information	Marketing and product placement	Product handling	Product information	Opinion research	Machinima	Opinion research
Education	Prevention and information	Society and relevant topics	Teacher education	Learning games	Science and recruiting	P2P learning models/ constructivism	Distance education /e-learning
Corporate	Worker health and education	Consumer education	Workers education	Continuing education and certificates	Advertising and visualization	Strategic planning	Work and process optimization
Industrial use	Operational safety	Operational safety	Workers education	Workers training	Simulation efficiency and optimization	Nano/bio-tech design	Work and process optimization

the past. Applications like dancing and fitness training or driver training are contributing to mobility preservation. Of special importance is the direct link between these learning and training sessions and the AAL system of the home. If an emergency occurs during the learning or training activity of the user, the system can identify the situation and start the necessary steps immediately. Especially with games requiring physical (training) activities, this functionality and the associated permanent provision of health care services are indispensable. These activity and skill games are based on practical relevance. Resulting is the task to match the requirements on a serious game for the elderly. These games should be easy to use, make fun, and provide a stimulating effect to maintain or even improve the existing skills "on the fly". Movements and reaction times are recorded by sensors, so the players can get an immediate feedback [9].

The greater challenge, however, lies in the learning of the basic operating concepts. In this area new, innovative, and age-appropriate games have to be developed allowing the elderly to playfully and easily learn the handling of their new technical systems. The technical foundations are laid by the assistance systems of Ambient Assisted Living. These are providing numerous possibilities. In the research project A^2LICE, these learning functions should be realized on tablet computers which are already used for building and equipment control in the homes of the elder people. This has some advantages. On the one hand, the users have to learn only the interaction with one device. On the other hand, many systems in the homes of the elder people, which were previously equipped with different operating concepts, partially inappropriate for the use by elder people, can be controlled in an easier way with the tablets. (For example, television remote control, temperature control, etc.).

5 Conclusions

Currently, researchers and developers are working in the interdisciplinary research field of human-system interaction to develop concepts for an intuitive, user-friendly design of interactive systems. The concepts are considering the findings of engineering and computer science disciplines as well as reflecting sub-disciplines of psychology, ergonomics, cognitive science, sociology and design [11].

The fundamental ideas of serious gaming are perfectly supporting learning in Ambient Assisted Living. The development of methods and supportive measures, particularly in the domain of rehabilitation and cognitive training, has just begun. Although some pilot projects in these areas exist, much fundamental research is needed, including acceptance research.

References

1. Leonhardt, S., Randow, A., Grünendahl, M., & Teich T. (2012). ESF-Forschungsprojekt Ambient Assisted Living zur Schließung der konzeptionellen Lücke in der medizinischen Versorgungskette zwischen stationärer Pflege und (kommunaler) Wohnungswirtschaft. In *Scientific Reports zur Konferenz Mobilität im Wandel —Nr. 3.* ISBN 978-3-9815433-2-2.
2. Garlipp, A., Künemund, H., Fachinger, U., & Erdmann, B. (2010). Auswirkungen der Einführung von technischen Assistenzsystemen – eine qualitative Studie, Working Paper Nr. 8, Zentrum Altern und Gesellschaft, Vechta.
3. Statistische Ämter des Bundes und der Länder. Demografischer Wandel in Deutschland, Heft 2. (2008).
4. Brach, J. S., & VanSwearingen, J. M. (2002). Physical impairment and disability: Relationship to performance of activities of daily living in community-dwelling older men. *Physical Therapy, 82*(8), 752–761.
5. Jakobs, E.M., Lehnen, K., & Ziefle, M. (2008). Alter und Technik, Studie zu Technikkonzepten, Techniknutzung und Technikbewertung älterer Menschen. Aachen: Apprimusverlag.
6. Bundesministerium für Bildung und Forschung (2008, August). Lebenslanges Lernen; in der Internet Archive-Version vom 22.
7. Tröger, S., Jentsch, D., Riedel, R., & Müller, E. (2012). Ernsthaftes Spielen—Eine Paradoxe Tätigkeit. In *Industrie Management 28*, 2012. GITO Verlag.
8. Plorin, D., & Müller, E. (2012). Serious game as an integral method for experimental research and professional knowledge transfer in the advanced learning factory (aLF): A conceptual approach for the practical use in the research project A^{2}LICE.
9. Zahn, F.A., & Senger, J. (2011). Dreimal täglich spielen - Wie Serious Games die Gesundheit älterer Menschen fördern können. In *Lernen im Alter – Hilfe zur Selbsthilfe.*
10. Hawlitschek, A. (2009). Spielend Lernen in der Schule? Ein Serious Game für den Geschichtsunterricht. http//www.spielbar.de/neu/wp-content/uploads/2009/06/hawlitschek_spielend_lernen.pdf
11. Weiniger, R., & Jäger, K.-W. (2010). Health & Exergames—Internationale Marktübersicht und Einsatzmöglichkeiten im AAL-Kontext; 3. Deutscher AAL-Kongress 26–27 Januar 2010. Berlin.
12. Loft, H. (2010). Serious Games: Märkte. Produzenten. Trends. Marktanalyse im Auftrag des Netzwerks Serious Games Berlin, 2010. Berlin.

Part II
Software Engineering Education Versus Industry Demand

Encouraging Transformational Learning and Reflective Practice with 2nd Year IT Students Using a Skills Inventory

Clive C. H. Rosen

Abstract Helping computing students acquire the skills employers require is fraught with problems. Students often do not see teaching these skills as a legitimate element of a computing curriculum. This chapter argues that part of the reason for this is a psychological resistance to self-exploration and self-evaluation and not the rational argument it appears to be. Furthermore, self-awareness is a pre-requisite for transformational learning which is pre-requisite for students being able to achieve their full potential. This chapter discusses the causes of student resistance to engaging fully in activities designed to improve their employability skills. It then discusses the concept of transformational learning as a common objective of higher education and preparation for employment. Finally, it presents the deployment of a skills inventory to introduce students to the concepts of self-evaluation and self-awareness which overcomes their natural ambivalence. Results have been encouraging and the student response positive.

Keywords Personal reflection · Personal development · Transformational learning · Skills development · Skills inventory

1 Introduction

An essential element in an industrial oriented education has to be equipping students with the skills employers expect of graduates. Consistently, when UK employers are asked about these skills, they respond by demanding a list of non-technical skills such as teamwork, communication skills, creativity and leadership [1]. Students on the other hand, tend to see these skills as peripheral, give little

C. C. H. Rosen (✉)
School of Computing and Mathematics, University of Derby, Derby, UK
e-mail: C.Rosen@Derby.ac.uk

G. Motta and B. Wu (eds.), *Software Engineering Education for a Global E-Service Economy*, Progress in IS, DOI: 10.1007/978-3-319-04217-6_7, © Springer International Publishing Switzerland 2014

regard to developing them, and fail to recognise activities associated with developing them as a legitimate part of the course.

Given such resistance to engaging in personal development type modules, finding ways of supporting student learning in this area in anything more than a superficial way is challenging. Simple compliance has little learning value. The goal needs to be personal reflection that leads to transformational learning [2, 3]. There is an essential qualitative difference between the experiencing, observing and reporting on experience, and the more profound personal insight required to help students achieve their true post graduate potential. Students often find it difficult to recognise this distinction.

The Skills Inventory presented in this chapter helps to provide a structured approach to achieving personal insight by focussing on the learning achieved from an experience.

2 Background

Reflective practice, as defined by Schön [4], is at the core of professional software systems development because technology changes so rapidly that intellectual agility is required to solve new problems based on previous experience. A key element that facilitates flexible thinking is confidence in our ability to solve problems and avoid psychologically damaging failure; a quality professionals have that neophytes tend to lack. Professionals acquire this faculty through the experience they acquire.

Self-confidence as distinct from technical knowledge cannot be gained from reading. As any practitioner would say, the manual cannot make up for real experience in doing the job, thinking about, and reflecting on how an activity could have been done better. Teague [5], Capretz [6] and others have found that computing students and professionals tend to score well above average on the Myers-Briggs personality inventory for both thinking and judging, suggesting that they would be less likely to value intuitive self-perception [7].

The concept of transformational learning derives from the ideas of cognitive modelling and constructionist psychology [8]. The suggestion here is that as we grow up, each person constructs a unique model of the world that enables them to make sense of their experiences. Brunner [9] identifies four ways in which this is achieved: by "negotiating and re-negotiating meaning" [9] with other people, by interpreting actions and events in context, by determining what is normal and by assuming the existence of rules and norms. Having established a conceptual understanding of the world through childhood, that construction is constantly challenged by new experience. Transformational learning is, in effect, the acceptance of that challenge in the face of the perceived security that one's current conceived world represents an inviolate understanding of the actual world. Transformational learning requires the constant reassessment and re-evaluation of the conceptual model by the individual.

Because a person's model is construed to include emotion and feeling, adjustments tend to require changes in self-perception which in turn require some self-awareness in the first place. So transformational learning incurs a personal "cost" which is the source of resistance to change or even the possibility of change. Rather than risk facing a potential threat to the existing model, a person might find ways to avoid the threat. Thus one might (and computing students often do) reject the notion that self-awareness is important, and a requirement to explore oneself, irrelevant to achieving one's personal objectives. The more insecure a person is in their personal identity, the more likely they are to resist invitations to explore themselves, thus making transformational learning less likely. Skills such as communication with others, leadership and teamwork touch the heart of our self perception because, as Brunner identified, interaction with others is how people generate their conceptual models (including concept of self) in the first place. The stereotypic computing student presents a greater challenge than students in other domains and hence a greater pedagogic challenge. They are generally reluctant to explore themselves or reflect on their personal skills.

The skills inventory presented here provides a less threatening way to begin the process of self reflection.

3 The Skills Inventory

The skills inventory presented here is a development from a skills matrix that was presented to the HEA BMAF Placements workshop in 2006. The inventory has evolved to its current version since that date. Six principles have emerged during this evolution:

1. To provide a supportive structure for student reflection.
2. To minimise the psychic threat to students.
3. To encourage students to identify specific examples to work on.
4. To focus on learning from personal experience.
5. To make the process of self-reflection intrinsic to the exercise.
6. To use the skills employers say they want as the vehicle for self-evaluation.

As can be seen in Table 1, each row represents one of the skills employers consider to be important. The student is asked to identify a specific example of when they have demonstrated each skill. If they have more than one example, they can insert additional rows under the same heading. The "activity description" column requires the students to articulate the specific circumstances. The "when" and "where" columns are included to ensure a particular time and place, and not a generalised activity. In the "what did you do" column, the word to emphasise is "you". People often experience these activities as part of a group, and it is important that students learn to differentiate themselves as an individual rather than simply a member of a group so that they can attribute the outcome to their personal contribution. Students are often reluctant to appreciate what they do well,

Table 1 Skills inventory

Skill	Activity description	When	Where	What did you do?	Outcome	Learning	Priority
Leadership/initiative taking							
Influencing/negotiating							
Team work							
Effective communication							
Self motivation							
Decision making							
Planning/organisation							
Working under pressure							
Personal development							
Commercial awareness							
Presentation/report writing							

and this helps them identify this. The seventh column, the "learning" column is the most important. It is these entries where the ideas of self-reflection and self-evaluation are expressed. Having the experience alone is insufficient. Professional development requires personal reflection on what has been learnt from the experience. To experienced professionals this may appear to be self evident, but to students and new entrants into the profession, the concept of continuous self-evaluation and reflection is novel.

The final column is optional. It is there to help students develop an action plan and to decide on which skills should be priorities for future development.

The inventory is not used as an abstract, stand alone exercise, but in conjunction with preparing to apply for placement or post graduate opportunities. UK employers commonly adopt a competency based approach to interviewing applicants (sometimes known as CAR, Context, Action, Result). This takes the form of asking such questions as 'describe a situation when.... what did you do.... what was the outcome?' The skills inventory helps prepare students for such questions and therefore improves their chances of performing well in interviews.

4 Outcomes

Students engaged well with this exercise. This was an assessed piece of work on a 2nd year B.Sc. Computing programme. In the past, in spite of setting personal reflection assignments such as reflective diaries, students have not engaged well, tending to concentrate on what happened, rather than analyse why a situation turned out the way it did. In this exercise, students presented some real insight.

- "I learnt to take each situation lightly and with care"
- "I learnt that each individual in the team had their own strengths and weaknesses"

- "I learnt and became more self confident"
- "[I] learnt how to talk to customers on a professional level"

The average mark for the exercise was 70 % (n = 29, sdev = 20) demonstrating that most students had been very thoughtful and taken the exercise seriously. It is clear that they put a lot of thought and effort into this assignment. The indications are that the skills inventory appears to have successfully introduced the students to self reflection and self-evaluation in a non-threatening way and avoiding the normal resistance that this type of exercise normally engenders.

5 Conclusions

Finding ways of helping computing students become self-reflective is challenging. They tend to see anything that is not strictly task oriented as a waste of time. Yet the role of most software and systems developers requires them to work in teams, take initiatives, be creative and so forth. Employers expect these skills and are often disappointed when graduates fail to demonstrate them. Employability needs to be put at the heart of the curriculum, and finding ways to overcome student resistance to engaging in non-technical learning is essential. This is intrinsically linked with becoming transformational learners because both require introspection, self-evaluation and self-awareness.

It was found that the use of reflective diaries or essays failed to provide sufficient structure to overcome students' conventional resistance. Students found it difficult to understand what was expected of them with these vehicles, concentrating on what happened rather than why. Reflective journals were not an effective way of encouraging the personal insight that leads to transformational learning.

The skills inventory has evolved over a period of time to provide a structured approach to personal reflection. This approach is less threatening and therefore more effective. It acts as a safer introduction to self-evaluation and has been used effectively to help prepare students for life in industry.

References

1. Assoc. of Graduate Recruiters (2010). AGR Manifesto. http://www.agr.org.uk/write/Documents/AGR_Manifesto_2010.pdf
2. Mezirow, J. (2000). Learning to think like an adult: Core concepts of transformation theory. In J. Mezirow & Associates, Learning as transformation: Critical perspectives on a theory in progress (pp. 3–33). San Francisco: Jossey-Bass.
3. Martin, J. (1989). *Information engineering* (Vol. 3). Prentice-Hall Inc.
4. Schön, D. (1991). *The reflective practitioner: How professionals think in action*. Arena: Aldershot.

5. Teague, J. (1998). Personality type, career preference and implications for computer science recruitment and teaching. In *ACSE*98, Australia: ACM.
6. Capretz, L. F. (2003). Personality types in software engineering. *International Journal of Human-Computer Studies, 58*(2), 207–214.
7. Myers, I. B., & McCaulley, M. H. (1985). *Manual: A guide to the development and use of the Myers-Briggs type indicator*. Palo Alto: Consulting Psychologists Press.
8. Kelly, G. A. (1991). *The psychology of personal constructs*. London: Routledge.
9. Brunner, J. (1990). *Acts of Meaning*. Cambridge: Harvard University Press.

Social Demand-Oriented Education Model for Software Engineering

Shu Liu, Lina Zhou, Peijun Ma, Dong Li and Shengchun Deng

Abstract With the rapid development of IT industry, a large number of software talents are urgent needed in China. However, according to the matter of fact, many graduate students have difficulty to find ideal jobs, while a lot of enterprises are suffering from a severe shortage of suitable talents. The traditional education model has been proved helpless in solving the contradiction between talent supply and demand. In this chapter, the software talent demands are analyzed, and a social demand-oriented education model for software engineering is proposed.

Keywords Social demand-oriented education model · Software engineering education · Software engineering curriculum · Industrial practice mechanism · Innovation training program

1 Introduction

With the coming of globalization and the age of information, software industry has become a new economy growth point all over the world. The development of software industry has very important strategic meaning for Chinese industrial

S. Liu (✉) · L. Zhou · P. Ma · D. Li · S. Deng
School of Software, Harbin Institute of Technology, Harbin, China
e-mail: sliu@hit.edu.cn

L. Zhou
e-mail: zln@hit.edu.cn

P. Ma
e-mail: ma@hit.edu.cn

D. Li
e-mail: Lee@hit.edu.cn

S. Deng
e-mail: dsc@hit.edu.cn

G. Motta and B. Wu (eds.), *Software Engineering Education for a Global E-Service Economy*, Progress in IS, DOI: 10.1007/978-3-319-04217-6_8, © Springer International Publishing Switzerland 2014

65

transition and upgrading. In 2010, the output of the software and information service industry increased to 18 % of the electronic information industry, and its employees over 3 million. The software industry revenue was more than 1.84 trillion RMB with an increase of 32.4 % in 2011, and more than 2.5 trillion RMB with an increase of 28.5 % in 2012. According to Chinese government's recently released report [1], by 2015, Chinese software industry revenue will exceed 4 trillion RMB and software exports will reach 60 billion Dollars. By then, 6 million software talents will be greatly needed in China.

In many Chinese colleges, the current education models for Software Engineering puts more emphasis on the basic theoretical knowledge, but neglect training the students' practice ability and professional quality, which lead to a big gap between the graduate's professional competence and the enterprises' requirements [2]. With such gap, many graduate students can hardly find an ideal job, while a lot of enterprises are suffering from a severe shortage of suitable talents. Obviously, the traditional education model is helpless in cultivating practice-oriented graduates, who could quickly fit into the industrial working environment. How to adjust the software engineering education model to meet the social demand is a big challenge for all the Chinese colleges.

2 Social Demand and Analysis

2.1 The Enterprises' Requirements

Investigations show that the practical talents urgently needed by the companies should have the following core professional competences [3, 4]:

(a) The talents should have a deep understanding of the solid software engineering knowledge, and be qualified for each specific work in the software development process.
(b) Strong programming skill and standard consciousness are essential for software talents. The graduates should be proficient in at least one programming language, such as the popular C language, C++, Java language, and also have the ability of composing the technical documentations.
(c) The talents should have good hands-on skills, be able to analyze, design and develop a small software system independently, and have certain actual project work experiences.
(d) Since the software industry is constantly changing and innovating, curiosity and consciousness are the basic conditions for the software talents to beat the competition.
(e) Team cooperation ability, good communication skills, independent learning ability, self-disciplined and enterprising spirit are the professional qualities required for the software talents.

2.2 The Graduates' Shortcomings

Enterprise investigations show that the graduates' basic knowledge is usually approved, but the practical ability and professional quality are not satisfactory and their general knowledge is limited. The problems can be summarized as follows:

(a) The graduates are usually weak at the range of knowledge and lack of comprehensive quality.
(b) Some of the programming technology is not practical and obsolete compared with the enterprises.
(c) Poor practical ability and lack of project experiences are the faults of most students.
(d) The learning initiatives and innovation consciousness are poor.
(e) The communication ability and team spirit also need to be improved [5].

2.3 The Reasons Causing the Gap

The causes for the gap between the graduates' qualities and the enterprises' requirements include four main factors [6]:

(a) Most of the colleges put more emphasis on the basic theoretical knowledge, but neglect the practice training.
(b) There is often a lag between the school curriculum and the enterprise application technologies.
(c) Isolated practice trainings cannot help the students digest all their learned knowledge.
(d) The curriculum lacks the courses related to soft skills cultivation such as communication skill, team work sprit, professional ethics and psychological resistant.

3 Social Demand-Oriented Education Model

To meet the talents demand, a social demand-oriented education model for software engineering is developed and adopted by the National Pilot School of Software at Harbin Institute of Technology (HIT-NPSS). The education model is shown in Fig. 1. In this model, basic knowledge acquisition, practice skills development, and innovation training are regarded as equally important.

As shown in Fig. 1, the model is composed of five categories: general education, professional education, practice training, innovation training and nonscheduled lectures.

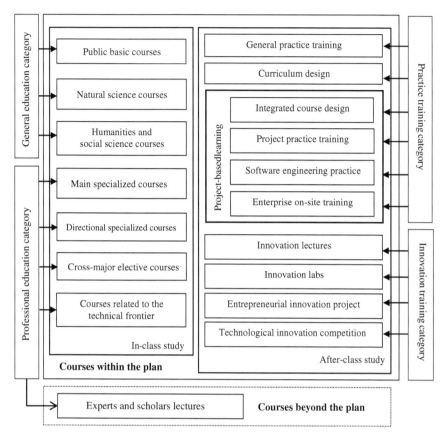

Fig. 1 Demand-oriented education model for software engineering

3.1 General Education Category

The purpose of general education is to provide opportunities for students to take courses that would broaden their education and challenge them by introducing them to areas outside of their major. The courses include Mathematics, English, Physical Education, Physics, Ideology Politics, Communication Skills, Marketing, Contract Law, Finial Management, IT Professional Quality and assorted.

3.2 Professional Education Category

Professional education aims to help the students master the software engineering knowledge and the programming skills. The courses can be divided into four groups:

(a) The main specialized courses cover the key content of the professional knowledge system, and can help the students develop a comprehensive understanding of the professional knowledge. The courses include Introduction to Software Engineering, Principle of Computer Organization, Database Systems and etc. Main specialized courses are compulsory and mainly offered in the first two school years.

(b) Directional specialized courses aim to strengthen students' specific professional skills. Four professional modules are designed based on the four popular application fields, which are Network Communications and Information Security module, Service Science and Enterprise Informatization module, Multimedia and Information Processing module, and Embedded System and Software module. Each module includes a series of specialized courses. At the beginning of the third school year, each student is required to select a module according to his interest.

(c) Cross-major elective courses are offered to widen the students' knowledge. Engineering Technology and Management are the two popular elective majors for software engineering students.

(d) Courses related to the technical frontiers are offered to avoid the lag between the school curriculum and the enterprise application technology, and broaden the student's vision and knowledge. These courses are designed based on the development of software technology.

3.3 Practice Training Category

Practice training aims to consolidate the knowledge learned from classes and develop their ability to settle down the real enterprise requirements. General practice training, Curriculum design, Integrated course design, Project practice training, Software engineering practice, and Enterprise on-site training are distributed throughout the four school years to train the students step by step. In this process, the students can learn the fundamental principles, activities, tools and best practices that are important building blocks of software engineering. In particular, the Enterprise on-site training requests the students to spend the final year in the companies and finish a real project based dissertation. The Enterprise on-site training provides a real chance for the students to participate in the industrial projects, be faced with the real business environment, real pressure, real project, real manager, and real work, and put the software theories and professional software engineering knowledge into use in the practical software designs and realization [7]. Practice training lays a solid foundation for the students to become qualified software engineers.

3.4 Innovation Training Category

Innovation training aims to improve the students' creativities and innovation consciousness. At the beginning of each semester, several innovation projects are provided to the students, and each student is encouraged to participate in a certain project according to his interest. Innovation lectures and labs are offered to support the students' innovation activities and the project must be finished in spare time. At the end of the semester, there will be a competition: the students shall demonstrate their outcomes, the innovation work will be evaluated, and the winner will be rewarded.

3.5 Experts and Scholars Lectures

These lectures are not in the course plan. Well-known experts, scholars and entrepreneurs home and abroad are invited to give students lectures occasionally. Advanced technology, new research findings, industry trends, enterprise development stories and even the popular topics may be the content. The tenet of the lectures is to animate campus atmosphere, wide the students' horizon and build the enterprises' image. Meanwhile, the lectures will promote the mutual understanding and extensive cooperation between enterprises and school.

4 Conclusions

Chinese software industry is developing fast. Talents majoring in software engineering are in great and urgent need. The traditional education model is no longer suitable for today's social economy environment. To narrow the gap between the graduates' qualities and the enterprises' requirements, we propose a social demand-oriented education model for software engineering. The new education model is recognized by the students and the enterprises, but cultivating enough excellent software engineers is still an arduous task.

References

1. Ministry of Industry and Information Technology of the People's Republic of China. (2012, April). The Twelfth Five-Year Plan of Software and information technology service industry. http://www.miit.gov.cn
2. Guoxiang, F., Guodong, S., Hao, C., & Peijun, M. (2007, February). On experience of industry-oriented education of software talents. The 2nd China Europe International Symposium on Software Industry Oriented Education. Ireland: Blackhall Publish.

3. Zhen, C. H., Bo, Z. H., & Kuangfeng, N. (2012). Software talent training plan based on the demand and the general occupation standard. *Computer Education, 7*, 57–59.
4. Weizeng, G., Guoyi, M., & Yuesheng, G. (2012). Research on personnel training model for software college according to industrial requirement. *Modern Computer, 16*, 41–43.
5. Shuang, L., & Pen, C. H. (2012). Adoption of employment-oriented experience training program to improve undergraduates employment competence. *International Journal of Modern Education and Computer Science, 4*(2), 52–58.
6. Jie, H., Qin, L., Zhen, G., Jianfeng, T., & Jinsong, F. (2011). A new model research and practice on training talents of software engineering based on university-industry cooperation. *Computer Engineering and Science, 33*(A1), 70–73.
7. Peijun, M., Shu, L., Jingchun, Xu., & Xiaofei, X. (2011, May). *The exploration and practice of university-enterprise collaboration in industrial practice: a factual instance of the excellent engineer plan. Proceedings of the 7th China-Europe International Symposium on Software Industry Oriented Education*. London, U.K.

Innovation and Practice of Engineering-Typed Talents Training Mode

Yi Qu, Xue-Qing Li, Ti Zhou and Li-Xin Li

Abstract Based on the problems occurring in recent years in the course of practical and engineering-typed software talents training of National Demonstration Software College of Shandong University, this chapter sums up the positive results of the College's "refined training mode" in the past few years and completes the simply intramural-oriented "refined training mode" in light of problems emerging in the development of new computer technology application and exceptional training orientation in contemporary society, exploring innovative joint training modes through integration of cultivation by universities and colleges, off-campus scientific research institutions and enterprise research centers and mainly through off-campus software studios supplemented by intramural ones.

Keywords Engineering-typed · Refined training · Joint training

1 Introduction

As a national demonstration college of software, Software College of Shandong University (SCSU) shoulders the mission of training intermediate and senior software talents in urgent need to meet the huge social demand in number as well as in quality for local information technology development [1]. Meanwhile the College should absorb the latest technical information of the field to cultivate high-quality

Y. Qu (✉) · X.-Q. Li · T. Zhou · L.-X. Li
Software College, Shandong University, Jinan, China
e-mail: quea@sdu.edu.cn

X.-Q. Li
e-mail: xqli@sdu.edu.cn

T. Zhou
e-mail: tzhou@sdu.edu.cn

L.-X. Li
e-mail: Lx@sdu.edu.cn

G. Motta and B. Wu (eds.), *Software Engineering Education for a Global E-Service Economy*, Progress in IS, DOI: 10.1007/978-3-319-04217-6_9,
© Springer International Publishing Switzerland 2014

engineering-typed talents in new technical areas. To achieve these goals, the College needs to update its training mode, to summarize its successful experiences in the process, to analyze problems emerging in the course of new social needs and talents training and to perfect the existing training mode while solving the problems.

As the establishment period of the National Demonstration Software Colleges expands and its training mode stabilizes, all those colleges have made active attempts in both the orientation and curriculum system and the training mode innovation of Master of Engineering [2, 3]. Taking actual situations of local areas and the colleges themselves into consideration, they gradually explore and form a series of training philosophies and orientations with distinctive features, which helps make considerable progress in training orientation of traditional software engineering, e-Government, digital media etc., and cultivate a myriad of outstanding engineering-typed talents for every walk of life.

In recent years, with the promotion and application of traditional technical in the field of new industries, Cloud Computing and Internet of Things have become a hot topic in contemporary society and relevant enterprises have launched their own products and services. The increase of social needs leads to huge expansion of demand for technical talents and engineering-typed talents, but how to train engineering talents in new fields that can meet the social needs? In the process of becoming National Demonstration Software College during the "Twelfth Five-year Plan period", it has to be considered how to achieve engineering talents and increasing social needs accessibility docking with joint help of scientific research institutes, enterprises and teacher force of various majors.

Currently, successful cases of joint training through cooperation among domestic scientific research institutes, relevant enterprises and universities abound. A case in point, Yuannan e-Government Network Management Center and Software College of Yunnan University opened a joint training in e-Government direction and achieved good results, due to which a specialized institute came into being—Yunnan e-Government Technology R&D Center. Located at Software College in Yangpu Campus, Yunnan University, the center mainly organizes professors and students of the college and people from various circles of society to undertake technical work, like e-Government Technology R&D, application and system simulation. At the same time, it also receives students from the college for professional practice, graduation design, and technology research and development.

In order to cultivate engineering talents in information security, Software College of Northeastern University builds close cooperation with enterprises and research institutions, like Neusoft Network Security Division and Liaoning Information Security Evaluation Center for engineering practices. Close attention are also paid to train students of their basic theoretical knowledge, practical ability of computer science and comprehensive quality highlighting the combination of theory and practice; of their ability to employ computer network technology, database technology, and information processing technology in computer information security, network security systems R&D and application. Students trained under this mode will be equipped with solid basic knowledge of mathematics and information security expertise, basic theories and methods of information science and technology and computer science and technology, strong ability of practical application, organization and coordination, teamwork spirit as well as competent programming capabilities.

In the past 2 years, relying on Liaoning Cloud Computing Engineering Technology Research Center, Software College of Northeastern University has carried out teaching and research in cloud security and has established specialized laboratory to work on virus attack and defense and information security. Software College of Beijing University of Aeronautics and Astronautics has also launched Master of Engineering training project in cloud computing direction, together with plenty of well-known enterprises and scientific research institutions home and abroad.

In terms of the training mode innovation, most Software Colleges have identified the philosophy of "highlighting engineering practice and cultivating students of their practical ability and innovative spirit" and have established the new iterative talent training mode of "learning over practice and practice-based learning and learning-based practice" with engineering practice as its core. For example, Software College of Beijing Jiaotong University adopts the teaching mode of "2 + 1 + 1" with practical course as its main line (viz., 2 years of full-time teacher in the college plus 1 year of specialized course teacher in enterprise plus 1 year of corporate internship); Software College of Shandong University takes the Refined Training Mode with "intramural software studio + off-campus training base" as its nucleus and supplemented by "learning guidance and career planning"; Software College of Huazhong University of Science and Technology employs software talent training chain mode of "elementary course—professional basic course—specialized course—practical course—engineering practice—graduation design"; Software College of Beijing Institute of Technology builds an intramural student innovation base with other enterprises; Hunan University implements "the teaching organizational mode of case driven 'learning over practice' and 'teaching as required'" with training students to be creative and teamwork as its main purpose.

Though making a series of accomplishments, Software Colleges are still faced with new problems. For example, how to improve the theory-oriented phenomenon in talents training? How to make better use of various research institutes and favorable resources of renowned enterprise to cultivate cutting-edge talents in current society? How to well combine intramural cultivation with off-campus training? All these are the key issues to be discussed in this chapter.

2 New Needs in Software Engineering Talent Training

In recent years, Software College of Shandong University (SCSU) has made long-term and beneficial attempts in the training of engineering and internationalized abilities of Master of Engineering. At present, SCSU's training mode has carried out continuous attempts, summaries and improvements of fields, like "software factory", "course training quality assurance system", "intramural and off-campus engineering training base construction" and has made a series of achievements, which are not only cheered by students, but also approved by employers, helping universities and colleges talents training satisfy social needs to certain extent.

However, at present, especially when new industries spring up, SCSU's training mode still has its weakness. The main issues are as follows:

2.1 How to Dock with Social Needs of New Industries

2.1.1 Teacher Force

For universities or colleges, teacher force is the priority for every major. Taking new industries, like Internet of Things and Cloud Computing as examples, the first concern of SCSU is how to establish strong teacher force with competent intramural teachers and those of off-campus research institutions integrated. For instance, Internet of Things major is a typical interdiscipline, involving professional knowledge of several majors, such as computer software and hardware, measurement and control, communication and the like, so it requires teachers of high quality.

2.1.2 The Hardware Construction

With the purpose of good achievements of talents training in new industries, National Demonstration Software Colleges have to lay emphasis on the hardware teacher construction, in addition to addressing teacher force issue. Still taking Cloud Computing and Internet of Things as examples, the core component of Internet of Things–Radio Frequency Identification (RFID) are only introduced in few universities, like Tsinghua University and Shanghai Jiaotong University. For Cloud Computing industry, if Software Colleges build its own Cloud, whether for application or for teaching, it requires a large investment, which is a problem to quite a few colleges and universities.

2.2 Training Mode Being Relatively Single

Most National Demonstration Software Colleges have formed a training mode of combining university teaching and corporate training. SCSU, for example, has been carrying on work in two aspects. Firstly, it established a college training center, consisting of 24 laboratories, like software technology laboratory, hardware technology laboratory, software engineering laboratory, database laboratory, media production laboratory, Linux based laboratories, e-home laboratory, e-Science Laboratory, e-Government laboratories, visualization technology laboratory, numerical pattern of the climate laboratory and Bochuang technology club and the like, in 4 categories, namely, laboratories of professional kind, new technology kind, engineering training kind and innovation kind. Those laboratories are used for fundamental, comprehensive and professional experiments and training students of intramural and off-campus graduation practice, new technology authentication, basic skills, pre-job training and open occupation training. Secondly, SCSU has built good cooperation with renowned international companies, like IBM, Intel, HP, Microsoft, Infor, E5 system, Citicorp Software and Technology Services (Shanghai) Co., Ltd. and NEC, and has built off-campus training base with over 50 famous companies home and abroad, like Digital China (China) Co., Ltd., Hisense Group, Langchao Group, Shanghai Wicresoft Co., Ltd. and Weihai Nongyou Software Co., Ltd.. These intramural and off-campus training bases do play a large role in training engineering-typed talents.

At the same time, however, with the rise of new industries, "intramural cultivation + enterprise training" mode has been proved unable to fully meet the needs of the new industries. SCSU needs to explore more effective training mode in order to better co-operate with qualified teacher resources in the field and to better complete high-level engineering-typed software talents training under the current situation.

2.3 Insufficient Cooperation Between Universities and Colleges and Social Scientific Research Institutions and Enterprises

Providing practical training prop for engineering-typed talents, enterprises occupies an important position in Software College's talents training and gives due support for docking between the colleges' talents training and social needs. Currently, enterprises, on one hand, cannot provide more resources for talents training, for they take industrialization features and profits as its priority; on the other hand, they do lack talents for new industries. This contradiction has become an obstacle in enterprise development.

Universities and colleges are stagnant in talents training due to their insufficient investment in a series of "soft" and "hard" prerequisites for new industries, like equipment, milieu, teacher force and curriculum system. At the same time, cooperation between universities and colleges and scientific research institutes and institutions and that between enterprise training and R&D centers are relatively weak, which are issues for universities and colleges to consider and try to address.

3 New Software Engineering Talent Training Mode

On the basis of the existing talents training mode, SCSU gradually implements new mode with "refined training" as its core. Considering the respective strengths and weaknesses of universities and colleges and enterprises, SCSU introduces

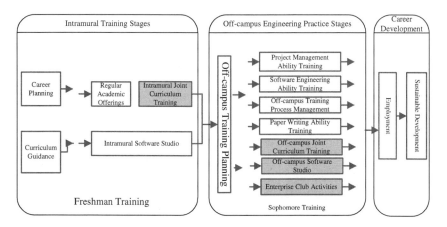

Fig. 1 The new software engineering talent training model

teachers from scientific research institutes and develops new mode in talents training for new industries [4–6]. This model is shown in Fig. 1.

As can be seen from Fig. 1, apart from intramural engineering capacity training, the "refined" training mode is also oriented towards simultaneous cultivation of abilities of actual engineering practice, project management, software engineering and comprehensive qualities with "real project" backing up. On the basis of the original training mode, the refined mode adds cooperation with research institutions of related industries, transferring independent college training to joint training mode between the college, research institutions and enterprises. In virtue of the favorable scientific research platform of research institutions and rich project resources of enterprises in new industries, the cultivation of engineering-typed talents will be completed together. After refinement, few following stages are added to the refined mode.

3.1 Joint Training Between Intramural and Off-Campus Curriculum

Joint training of the curriculum is a core part of the teaching resources of scientific research institutions brought in by SCSU. Investing a lot in plenty of new industries at home, research institutions have built necessary research platforms and are quite capable of training talents. If these resources can be integrated with universities' cultivation, huge progress can be made for the current engineering-typed talents training. At present, main orientation arrangements of joint training introduced by SCSU can be viewed in Table 1.

Table 1 Main orientation arrangements

Training orientation	Main courses
Mobile cloud computing orientation	Introduction to mobile cloud computing, mobile cloud computing server technology, mobile cloud computing development technology engineering practice, virtualization technology, etc.
Software testing and evaluation orientation	Evaluation object business analysis, system architecture analysis, system technology analysis, system implementation analysis, testing process analysis, testing defect analysis, cloud testing, etc.
System integration orientation	Computer simulation, introduction to cim system, demonstration and optimization of complex network system, concurrent engineering and knowledge management, enterprise information system principle and engineering, etc.
Internet marketing and management orientation	Introduction to internet marketing, SEO/SEM engineering practice, online consuming behavior analysis, internet marketing frontier and development, etc.

3.2 Intramural and Off-Campus Software Studio

Through the in-depth cooperation with off-campus scientific research institutions and enterprises, the focus should be shifted on off-campus software studio on the basis of the establishment of intramural studio. Project training in off-campus studio should be strengthened given that intramural curriculum time is reasonably arranged [7].

In view of training form, intramural and off-campus software studios take the "project courses" form, which refers to software studio, that is, software development project as well as credit courses. Students, who meet the requirements of completing the actual project development, will get due credits. In terms of orientation arrangement, SCSU divides its internal studio into 3 major and 7 minor categories, and the details can be seen as follows:

- Software studio of technical kind includes studios of J2EE, NET and test.
- Software studio of outsourcing kind includes studio outsourcing to Japan and Europe and America.
- Software studio of embedded kind includes the embedded hardware and software studios.

In the meantime, universities and colleges and social scientific research institutions build close co-operation and 4 off-campus software studios will or be planned to be added recently. The off-campus software studio after the addition is shown in Fig. 2.

Intramural and off-campus software studios are established based on software engineering development concept, where students undertake the whole process from requirements capture and analysis, architecture design, database design to

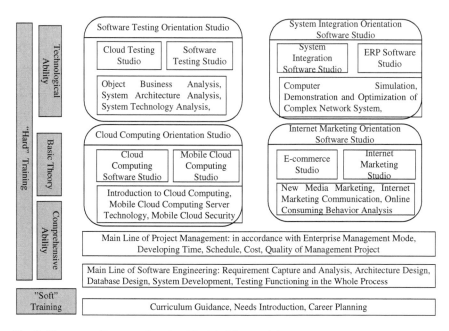

Fig. 2 The new software engineering talent training model

system development, system deployment and testing. At the same time, students are supervised in accordance with the mode of enterprise management so as to train students of their comprehensive capacity. Students in the studios mainly engage in actual project development training, while practical theory explanation will be exposed to them by the guiding team.

In terms of talents training of new industries currently, off-campus software studios are more and more important owing to the soft and hard investment of scientific research institutions. The talents training mode of mainly through off-campus software studio and supplemented by intramural software studio has been established. The two types of software studio together constitute the main positions in the SCSU engineering-typed talents training.

3.3 Enterprise Club Activities

Perfected Refined Training Mode expands its cooperation with enterprises, adding main joint training details, like team development training and enterprise project investigation and exchange, setting up jointly the students' consultation platform and project research cooperation.

4 Initial Success of Management Innovation

In recent years, SCSU actively pursues management mode innovation matching "refined" training, which has achieved good results in Master of Engineering training, especially in strengthening students' engineering ability. It can be mainly shown in the following aspects.

First, in terms of curriculum system construction, the original courses classification has been refined. In light of the new industries, curriculum system of related majors has been built. Several backbone courses have been introduced in new majors around Cloud Computing, Internet of Things, software testing and evaluation and system integration and over 10 relevant courses are being brought in and built. The new courses broaden students' horizon, and win welcome and praise from students and the community.

Second, in terms of the combination with social educational resources, SCSU pays great attention to deep cooperation with relevant social scientific research institutions, in addition to joint training with related enterprises in engineering-typed talents cultivation. SCSU currently builds off-campus training base and software studio with enterprises and scientific research institutions leading, which function as strong complement to theoretical courses in school and campus software studio and share high-level engineering software talents training. So far, 5 intramural and off-campus studios have been set up one after another, which play its due role in students' development.

Third, in terms of talents cultivation flow management, information system has been integral support for "refined" training and management, due to which management efficiency and accuracy of Master of Engineering have been greatly improved. Meanwhile, "refined" management philosophy also caused students' great concern of the whole training process, besides, communication and interaction between on-job Master of Engineering and SCSU and their supervisors has been greatly improved.

After preliminary exploration and practice, Master of Engineering in SCSU do make obvious progress in their comprehensive quality and vision and their abilities of engineering practice, project management, career planning, chapter writing as well as their adaptability of new industries and better complete SCSU's training philosophy and mission.

5 Conclusion

With the exploration of engineering training mode and management mode in recent years, SCSU objectively summarizes the new problems in the original training mode, and actively makes attempts for new social needs, proposing the refined training mode that universities, enterprises and scientific research institutions work together to satisfy social needs, and then making appropriate improvement and completion [8, 9]. In the meantime, SCSU focuses on attempts and innovation of the relevant management mode to achieve its training philosophy.

Though these new modes provide solutions to emerging issues, we should be aware that any method cannot solve all problems. As society develops and new industries emerge, SCSU will strengthen docking between engineering-typed talents training and social needs to make its achievements more satisfactory.

References

1. Software College Promotes Chinese Software Talents to the World–Interview with Joan Chen, Chinese Software Industry Association. http://www.guanliguancha.com/show.asp?id=162
2. Training Program of Master of Engineering in the Field of Software Engineering (revised).
3. Final Report of National Demonstration Software College Acceptance of Shandong University, unpublished document of Software College of Shandong University.
4. Meng, X., Li, X., & Quyi. Exploration into engineering-typed talent training mode. In *The second China–Europe International Symposium on Software Industry Oriented Education Edition.*
5. Meng, X., Li, X., Quyi. Innovation and quality guarantee system of engineering talent training mode. In *The 3rd China–Europe International Symposium on Software Industry Oriented Education.*
6. Quyi., Meng, X., Li, X. Exploration and innovation of engineering software talent refined training mode. In *The third China–Europe International Symposium on Software Industry Oriented Education Edition.*
7. Management Measures of Software Studio Implementation of Software College of Shandong University (Trial), unpublished document of Software College of Shandong University, Jinan.
8. Ideal and Practical Issues of Software College and its Countermeasures. http://news.csdn.net/n/20061115/97582.html
9. Zhang Y. (2004). Reflection on the foundation of mode software colleges. *Chinese Higher Education 10.*

Enterprise Oriented Software Engineering Education: A Framework for Employability

Gianmario Motta, Daniele Sacco and Linlin You

Abstract In order to comply the need of innovation and high quality of the more and more demanding request of enterprises, universities should manage the quality of services and the quality of contents. We illustrate a framework for a graduate curriculum in Software Engineering, that is aimed to maximize employability in a global world. The framework defines the quality measures, the process of managing the quality and the approach to a curriculum that reflects the needs of the enterprises.

Keywords Higher education · Service quality · Software engineering education

1 Introduction

The global competition is pushing the quest for excellence in universities. In general terms, according to the ranking made by Times [1], top university should excel in the following areas:

1. Teaching: the learning environment
2. Research: volume, income and reputation
3. Citations: research influence
4. Industry income: innovation
5. International outlook: staff, students and research

G. Motta (✉) · D. Sacco · L. You
Department of Industrial and Information Engineering, University of Pavia,
Pavia, Italy
e-mail: motta05@unipv.it

D. Sacco
e-mail: daniele.sacco01@ateneopv.it

L. You
e-mail: linlin.you01@ateneopv.it

G. Motta and B. Wu (eds.), *Software Engineering Education for a Global E-Service Economy*, Progress in IS, DOI: 10.1007/978-3-319-04217-6_10,
© Springer International Publishing Switzerland 2014

Other rankings consider slightly different areas. E.g. the Top Ranking web site uses a quality scale that includes Employability, Facilities, Innovation, Access, Research, Teaching, Internationalization and, finally, ad hoc criteria concerning the subject area [2].

However such excellences are not equally important for everybody. If excellence in research is an attraction factor for professors, excellence in teaching, services and internationalization are attraction factors for students. Furthermore, for a software engineering master student, employability is probably the critical factor. Employability implies high quality in teaching and a close relationship with enterprises, which are the end customer of software engineering. On the other side, an international approach to teaching is essential in a global world.

Our purpose is to sketch out a reference framework for employability that addresses Master of Science (MS) degree in Software Engineering (SE).

Let us clarify the "employability" perspective. SE graduates have to fit a variety of employment opportunities, that range from systems integrator and large user enterprises to software houses, as we suggest in Fig. 1. Therefore, SE contents shall ideally encompass a variety of perspectives, as Enterprise Architecture, Database, Service Engineering and alike.

Also, a good reference framework should produce a competitive higher education not only in educations contents but also in education quality. In our view, education quality includes two main areas, namely service quality and content quality.

The quality of educational services is illustrated in Sect. 2, that proposes the widely known SERVQUAL model. Section 3 illustrates how to manage the quality of service, and proposes a framework based on the best practices of Service Level Management (SLM). Section 4 is on the quality of contents; it proposes a two phases education, respectively on foundations and industry-related projects; it is aimed to the cooperation with enterprises. Section 5 sketches out a possible process to manage contents on a global basis. Finally, conclusions summarize the proposal and identify future steps. The quality areas are summarized in Fig. 2.

2 Service Quality: Measurement

Undoubtlessly education is a service and the quality of service is an attraction factor of students. With over 10,000 quotations, SERVQUAL [3, 4] is the gospel for measuring the quality of services. The quality is measured through a multi-item scale, that assesses the quality perceived by customers [3]. The SERVQUAL model (Fig. 3) shows that the quality involves various stakeholders with different viewpoints, namely management and consumers, who may have opposite views (and often do). SERVQUAL is easily adapted to measure the quality of education services as we exemplify in Table 1.

What are the domains of service quality in higher education? In general terms they include (a) activities that run within university premises and (b) activities on or relations with the external environment, such as cooperation with enterprises. A

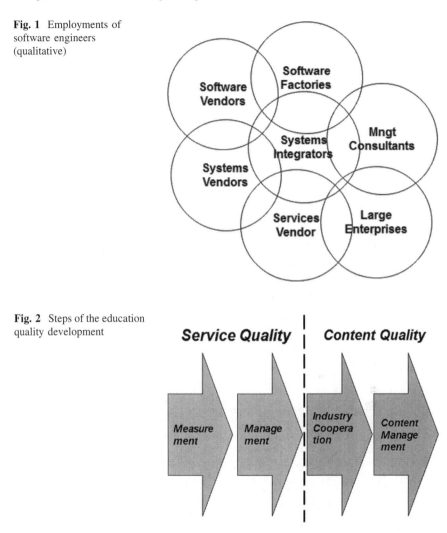

Fig. 1 Employments of software engineers (qualitative)

Fig. 2 Steps of the education quality development

summary of service domains is given in Table 1. Let us notice that pure academic research, as publishing scientific papers or projects funded by the government, is not included in the domains of critical services.

3 Service Quality: Management

Of course, quality has to be managed (Table 2). For this purpose, we propose a framework emerging from IT management. In the domain of IT management, comprehensive quality frameworks have been developed. For, the service quality is a critical issue in IT management, where enterprises buy several critical IT

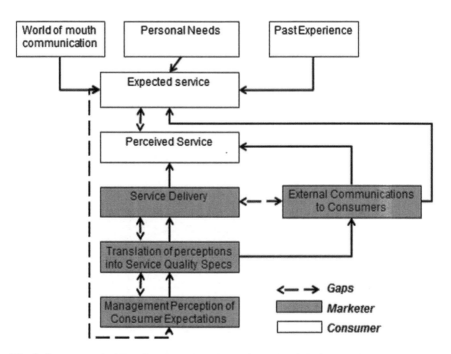

Fig. 3 Parasuraman's SERVQUAL model, adapted from the original paper [3]

Table 1 The SERVQUAL gaps customized to higher education (adapted from [20])

Original SERVQUAL gaps	Adaption to EDUCATION SERVICES
Management perception of consumer expectation versus consumer expectations	Student expectations versus university perceptions on student expectations
Management perception of consumer expectation versus service quality specs	Authority perceptions of student expectations and service (teaching) quality specs
Service quality specs versus service delivered	Service quality specs and service delivered
External communications to consumers versus service delivery	Service delivery versus the promised teaching outcomes to students
Perceived services versus expected service	Student's expectation versus perception

services e.g. network services. In this context, the service quality is defined by customers in a framework called SLA (Service Level Agreement) [5], as an addendum to the service contract. The SLA defines the quality measures of the service to be supplied and states the penalties to be applied if the contract promise is not fulfilled. An overall profile of a SLA is given in Table 3.

The customer not only states the quality objectives, but also plans, monitors, controls and continuously improves the quality of service received through a cycle called SLM (Service Level Management). SLM is described in global IT management practices as ITIL [6], COBIT [7] and, for development services, CMMI [8]. In this context, the provider shall balance resource efficiency and service

Table 2 Quality aspects in education (adapted from [20])

Quality aspect	Description
Campus services	Physical facilities, equipment, support services and attraction of campus
Customer care	Care of students (assistance, tutorship, etc)
Teaching content	The scientific quality of the content and the quality of delivery
Brand	Outplacement, visibility, image
Industry cooperation	Consulting, research, internships and joint projects
International cooperation	Joint university program, agreements, faculty

Table 3 SLA profile (adapted from [5])

Item	Description
Purpose	Objectives to achieve by using a SLA
Restrictions	Necessary steps or actions to be taken to ensure that the requested level of services are provided
Validity period	SLA working time period
Scope	Services to be delivered to consumers, and services not to be covered in the SLA
Parties	Involved organizations or individuals and their roles
Service-level objectives (SLO)	Levels of services which parties agree. Service level indicators (e.g. availability, performance, reliability) apply
Penalties	Amount of compensation to the customer that is to be applied if delivered service does not achieve SLOs
Optional services	Not mandatory services that can be requested
Administration	Business processes to guarantee the achievement of SLOs and the related organizational responsibilities for controlling

quality, a critical challenge in the current age of cloud services [9, 10]. In short, a SLM system would typically include three elements [11, 12]:

- The variables that specify the quality of service, and that are included in SLA-like definition of services to students;
- The systems and procedures that measure the actual quality and compare it against the expected quality, thus assessing the quality gap;
- The organizational roles to manage SLM and SLA.

The last point is critical in an university. While, within an enterprise, multiple provider organizations supply services to one customer organization, i.e. the enterprise, in the university landscape one provider organization (i.e. the university itself) supplies services to multiple customers/stakeholders such as students, government, enterprises. Given this multiplicity, the formal SLA of enterprises has to be replaced by a set of statement/promise of service, that shall be differentiated according to the different classes of customers/stakeholders. The grid of Table 4 describes the potential activities of each actor in such SLM-like framework; the "Comment" column explains their role within the grid.

Table 4 A grid of SLM-like roles for university

Actor	Activity in SLM /SLA system	Comment
University management	It plans, monitors and controls service level objectives (SLO) and undertakes actions to enhance efficiency (cost) and effectiveness (quality delivered)	University management is the only actor which can develop an overall SLA/SLM, though it is a provider
Professors and university services	They supply services to students	Professors (and university services) are service suppliers and hardly they have the time needed for a SLM system
Students	They receive and partially assess the services (survey on students, focus groups)	Students have not the authority nor the organization needed for SLA/SLM
Enterprise	They can cooperate by panels and focus groups in defining the expected service level	Enterprises use the outcome of the universities, namely students and projects, and have the organization needed for stating SLA/SLM, but they lack of a real competence on education
Government and/or foundation	They state overall expected performances	Government can (and sometimes do) define SLA-like statements, but it is the funding organization of the university rather than its user

Fig. 4 The two phases
learning model

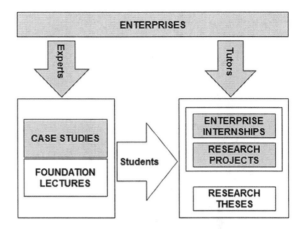

4 Content Quality: Industry Cooperation

Education contents are a key element of quality and a critical point for employ-ability. Would you ask most Software Engineering students what they are looking for, they would answer "a good job". In this perspective, the value of an university is the ability of enabling students to find a good job, i.e. to graduate students which fit the request of enterprises. Therefore, contents and teaching shall be as close as possible to industry needs. Students should not only know software engineering theory but also how to develop software, and, even more critical, how to identify and implement innovative applications. This issue has been addressed in CEISEE papers that propose industry oriented curricula both in Europe [13–15] and China [16].

According to this view, master students typically spend one year on foundation courses and one year on projects, that reflect industry issues, with teachers who are industry experts. We call this a two-phase learning model. The first phase is aimed to lay down theoretical foundations, while the second phase is aimed to develop industry oriented competences. An overall schema of the model is given in Fig. 4 where the filled squares indicate a substantial involvement of the enterprises. Let us explains the individual elements of the model, namely case-studies, internships, research projects, research theses.

Case-studies are project works, made by student teams or individually, that aim to solve an enterprise problem e.g. students have to redesign a workflow of a mortgage loan service of a bank, going through the whole software lifecycle, form analysis to implementation. The problem has to be a real issue in a real enterprise, and is described by a text and/or testimonials. The case study is particularly effective with reviews and walkthroughs at each stage of the project—e.g. anal-ysis, design, implementation, user test etc. This approach enables students, as in Harvard case-method [17], to accumulate experience, without leaving the pro-tected environment of the university. Case-studies, although give only simulated and not real life experience, push students to test theory.

Table 5 Industry-oriented approaches

Level	Cost to university	Return to university	Cost to enterprises	Return to enterprises
Case study	High: massive tutorship	Low: marginal knowledge acquisition	Low: testimonials and support materials	High: students get prepared to project activities
Enterprise internships	Low	Higher with joint projects	Low	High
Research thesis	High: faculty involvement	Potentially high: state-of-art advances	Variable	Potentially high: more theoretical knowledge

Internships typically imply a stage of six month to one year in an enterprise in which students perform a practical assignments. Internships enable students to accumulate real life experience, but they lack the continuous tutorship that support case-studies. Moreover, effective internships require careful planning to select enterprises, assignments and students and, also, a concurrent quality control by university tutors. The internship may be performed not only in projects run by the enterprises but also in joint or research projects where the project team encompasses both university and enterprises staff. From students' view point these internships can be considered a special case of regular enterprise internships, but from university viewpoint they increase knowledge.

Finally, research theses address state-of-art issues or topics in innovative fields as cloud computing, big data and alike. These theses, traditionally given to doctoral students, are suitable for best master students. In our experience, master students who have been involved in research projects can get better jobs and faster career. Also, the higher the level the higher the return to the University—it is a win-win business.

In Table 5 we summarize the cost, expressed in terms of hours spent, and the return, measured by a quality scale of knowledge acquisition, of each approach. Surprisingly, the case-study level has a very high cost, but, as Harvard shows, gives the highest preparation. While a an industry oriented curriculum is a common objective, the reality is often quite limited, as you can see from the research made by Choudaha [18].

5 Content Quality: Management

The wide demand and the deep competence needed for each subject require huge resources. These, in our view, are beyond the scope of most individual universities. Hence, either universities focus on a specific set of industry and competences or, while maintaining such focalization, cooperate in a common industry oriented approach, thus enhancing also internationalization. A free cooperation agreement or informal consortium looks suitable for so different contexts as China and Europe. Three key elements can be identified: strategy, operations, technology.

Strategy will identify not only overall long term objectives but also the product and the underlying organization. The product strategy includes the portfolio of student competences to be developed, related syllabi, and industry collaboration projects. The organization strategy defines the roles of participating universities and (hopefully) enterprises.

Operations are the activities and the organization needed to run such agreement, that implies reference points in each university, and operational agreement as student and professor exchange. The exchange template can include Double Master Program as the one being run by HIT, UESTC and Tongji University with the University of Pavia [19]. Incidentally, such programs can also enhance internationalization of participating universities.

Technology includes the systems to support the common approach, and they include a common knowledge base with teaching material and learning technologies.

6 Conclusions

The globalization and continuing innovation of software applications are demanding high quality graduates, who not only know software theory but also are able to develop innovative applications. Within these perspective, we have sketched a framework for an industry oriented curriculum, that targets graduate students. The framework assumes that, while the quality of services is an important attraction factor, the quality of curricula is essential for a high employability, and, last not least, to help industries to develop innovation. In order to have high quality curricula two levels of cooperation are needed, on one side between universities and enterprises and, on the other side, across universities.

References

1. http://www.timeshighereducation.co.uk/
2. http://www.topuniversities.com/qs-stars/rating-universities-specialist-subjects-qs-stars
3. Parasuraman, A., Berry, L. L., & Zeithaml, V. A. (1985). A conceptual model of service quality and its implications for future research. *J. Mark., 49*(4), 41–50.
4. http://istheory.byu.edu/wiki/SERVQUAL
5. Raimondi, F., Skene, J., Emmerich, W. (2008). *Efficient online monitoring of web-service SLAs: Proceedings of the 16th ACM SIGSOFT International Symposium on Foundations of Software Engineering.* ACM.
6. http://www.itil-officialsite.com/
7. ISACA, COBIT 5. (2012). http://www.isaca.org/cobit/Documents/
8. SEI (Software Engineering Institute). (2010, November). CMMI for development, version 1.3, technical report, http://www.sei.cmu.edu/reports/10tr033.pdf

9. Ferretti, S., et al. (2010). *Qos–aware clouds. Cloud computing (CLOUD): 2010 IEEE 3rd International Conference on IEEE.*
10. Liu, X, et al. (2011). *A generic QoS framework for cloud workflow systems. Dependable, autonomic and secure computing* (DASC): *2011 IEEE Ninth International Conference on. IEEE.*
11. Motta, G., Barroero, T., Galvani, F., Longo, A., (2011) *IT service level management: Practices in large organizations*, IBIMA Publishing, Communications of the IBIMA, http://www.ibimapublishing.com/journals/CIBIMA/cibima.html, Vol. 2011 (2011), Article ID 635464, 12 pages, doi: 10.5171/2011.635464.
12. Barroero, T., Motta, G., Pignatelli, G., Longo, A., Bochicchio, M., Raffone, R. (2010). *Aligning IT service levels and business performance: A case study*, SCC.
13. Motta, G., Barroero, T., Sacco, D. (2012). *Modeling user needs as enterprise analysts*, CEISIEE.
14. Motta, G., Barroero, T. (2011). *Teaching High Level Information Requirements-A case study on a successful undergraduate course*, CEISIE.
15. Motta, G., Pignatelli G. (2010). *Services Engineering curriculum: a case study, CEISIE.*
16. Meng, X., Li, X., Qu, Y. (2006). *Exploration into engineering-typed talent training mode: The second China—Europe International Symposium on Software Industry Oriented Education Edition.*
17. http://www.hbs.edu/teaching/inside-hbs/
18. Choudaha, R. (2008). *Competency-based curriculum for a master's program in service science, management and engineering (SSME)*: An online Delphi study (Doctoral Dissertation, University of Denver, 2008).
19. http://eecs.unipv.it/degrees/computer-engineering/
20. Babiarz, P., Piotrowski, M., Wawrzynkiewicz, M., Malgorzata. (2003). *The application of service quality gap model to evaluate the quality of blended learning*: IADIS International Conference e-Society 2003.

Rethinking the Talents Cultivation Mode of Software Engineering

Dongming Chen, Zhiliang Zhu and Dongqi Wang

Abstract China's economy continues to develop, the process for all walks of life gearing to international standards speeds up. As an important aspect of information technology, software engineering has already gotten high attention from all sides. Universities are the main training institution for cultivating advanced software talents, they are shouldered with the mission of training software talents who meet the requirements of the society. Software industry is a strong support for China's national economy. How to strengthen and improve software engineering talents cultivation directly relates to development of information technology or even the economy of the whole society. This paper rethinks software engineering talents cultivation from specialty construction, innovative talents training, education of the age of big data, internationalization and excellent engineers plan.

Keywords Software engineering · Talents cultivation · Internationalization · Excellent engineer education plan · Big data

1 Introduction

Responding to the calling of the Ministry of education of China, the National Pilot Software College of China actively carry out the education reform of software engineering, relieve the contradiction between the recruitment dilemma of employing unit and the difficult employment of graduates, and so promote better development of information technology industry of China. It has been done by

D. Chen (✉) · Z. Zhu · D. Wang
Software College, Northeastern University, Shenyang, China
e-mail: chendm@mail.neu.edu.cn

Z. Zhu
e-mail: zhuzl@swc.neu.edu.cn

G. Motta and B. Wu (eds.), *Software Engineering Education for a Global E-Service Economy*, Progress in IS, DOI: 10.1007/978-3-319-04217-6_11,

changing the traditional teaching idea, reforming of traditional teaching system and curriculum, developing school-enterprise cooperation, construction of double-quality teacher team and promoting international exchange and cooperation. Though these measures have achieved good results, there are still some problems. The following describes the problems that we should rethink for software engineering talents cultivation.

2 Rethinking Problems

2.1 Expansion of Software Engineering Discipline

2.1.1 Opportunities and Challenges of Software Engineering

The establishment of first-grade state subject of software engineering brings new opportunities as well as some challenges, such as how to improve the quality of software engineering education, heighten the training quality of software engineering talents, fasten promoting the level of scientific research in software engineering, enhance the software engineering community service abilities, optimize structure to obtain subject characteristics and create first-class disciplines of a world-class university. We should think it over on the following aspects to expand software engineering discipline:

1. Compared with the first-class discipline, what is missing from the discipline of software engineering;
2. To cultivate students' interest in software engineering discipline;
3. Teaching mode and discipline system reform;
4. To cultivate compound talents with multiple channels;
5. Reasonable evaluation and assessment system of academic;
6. Investigation and thinking of the industry (Enterprises full participate in talents training).

2.1.2 The Road of Professional IT of a New Generation of Software Engineering

Something must be done to overcome students' impetuous style of study, to cultivate students' professional level and practical ability, to lead the new generation students correctly looking at the development of software engineering industry, to realize that the cooperation between University and enterprise promotes education and innovation. Thus the following four measures should be taken into consideration:

1. Clutching at both ends, so the middle. Solid work must be employed to improve professional education and graduates employment guidance as well as professional and technical level.
2. Go deep into the docking of talents training and market demand. Enhancing the joint between schools and enterprises and setting the training objectives for the market.
3. Cultivate creative talents with high level and good practical ability. Improve the curriculum construction and teaching reform of the first class (in the classroom), at the same time, give full play to the second class (outside the classroom).
4. Strengthen discipline cross to enhance features. Cross software engineering courses to other subjects, indraught advanced courses from abroad, push ahead the cooperation between university and industry and invite experienced engineers to teach in school, encourage the students independently to start their own business.

2.2 Innovative Talents Cultivation

2.2.1 Innovative Talent Localization

In addition to the big stage of the society, the main bases of talents cultivation are universities. Before the graduates get into the society, the employing units have already expected the students' innovative ability, that is too say, it is the universities who play the most important role for training the students' innovative ability. So, it is very necessary to construct the innovative university.

Innovative talents cultivation depends on teamwork and group creation. A successful team must consider the following four aspects: (1) Selecting correct direction, focusing on the first class scientific and applicable problem; (2) Gathering talents in one place and forming composition of forces for scientific research; (3) Platform construction and establish research bases with precise equipment and excellent environment; (4) Target setting and task allocating, aiming at scientific leading edge and national significant requirement.

Innovative talents should possess broad field of vision, the most important is opening mentality which includes competitive idea, collaborative consciousness, global opinion, thoroughly understand international regulations as well as intercultural communication and problem solving ability.

In the past 15 years, many outstanding talents were imported from overseas or trained domestically.

Close attention should be paid to sustainable development of the innovative talents. We must make a loose, free and harmonious environment for innovative talents growing to maturity.

2.2.2 Innovation and Entrepreneurship Education

For software engineering students, we think the talents cultivation mode of IT Innovative Studio should be advocated, which combines classroom teaching and real project to train software talents who possess creative spirit and the ability to meet the needs of the society [1].

1. Basic condition for IT Innovative Studio

(a) Set up perfect administration mechanism to keep highly effective running;
(b) Build up high quality students group and teaching staff;
(c) Enhance propagandas to erect brand influence;
(d) Establish comfortable software and hardware environment to construct favorable working atmosphere.

2. Measures for the implementation process

(a) Keep up with the times for software engineering curriculum revolution;
(b) Construct innovative practice platform and students selecting system with the carriers of enterprise project development or competition;
(c) Build up good real project environment;
(d) Put project driven teaching into practice;
(e) Structure diversified teaching evaluation system.

2.3 Software Engineering Education of the Age of Big Data

2.3.1 Challenges of Big Data

With the development of mobile Internet and Web2.0, data size is dramatically increased [2], and the next 10 years will be an intellectual science and technology era leaded by big data [3].

The coming of big data is a heavy blow to mankind. The influence spreads everywhere and of course, software engineering education is also not an exception.

Under such background, software engineering education is faced with the following challenges:

- Transformation of computing thinking and cognition pattern [4];
- Massive learners and supplementary teaching resources [5];
- Basic requirements for software engineering talents were changed.

2.3.2 Consideration on Software Engineering Education

1. The adjustment of discipline contents. How to cultivate software engineering talents catering to big data research is a challenge. We called the talents data scientists which will be a kind of new-style talents in the next ten years.
2. Transformation of talents requirement.
3. Evaluating teachers' cultivation and qualities.
4. Exploration and practice.

2.3.3 Cloud Computing and Transparent Computing

Though the cloud campus in some universities provides many conveniences to the students, it cannot flexibly combine education resources of other companies and other universities. Prof. Yaoxue Zhang, academician of Chinese Academy of Engineering has proposed a concept and model called transparent computing, for future computation in the world. Transparent computing let a user terminal just preserve some very basic functions. According to different requirements, various system functions and applications can be downloaded from servers piece by piece in a flow way [6].

Let's make a bold imagination to apply the model "transparent computing" to running universities, and realize "transparent university", with the features, (1) The university just keep minimal functions, e.g., designing curriculum system, managing and supervising education activities, and organizing the evaluation of faculties and students; (2) Faculty and various industry experts make contacts of education with university as education providers; (3) Establishing and promoting policies for credits, qualifications, and standardization in the world for various education activities.

Through transparent university, we can have the following benefits. (a) Change of education service model: students do not need to mind the location of campus, educator and course. According to their requirement, the students can find the corresponding education provider and courses. (b) Promoting mutually merging of various campus and education system, also including university and company for education: In a university, there can be different curriculum systems from multiple universities. Cultivation courses of companies can be merged into the course systems. Students or faculties can study and work across different universities arbitrarily. (c) Open education system setting and education management: making various interfaces and standards between universities and education service providers (professors and experts), bridge the gap of education environment and services.

2.4 Unique Talents Training/Compound Talents Training

Degree of automation in many industries (e.g., metallurgy, finance, etc.) is gradually raising, and the professional requirement in these industry is also changed. The requirement for industry informatization talents is increasing, especially for software talents [7, 8].

The levels of informatization in different industries are varied, and there are still specificity in some industry, e.g., metallurgical. These special industries have active demand for talents who are familiar with software engineering technology, possess the ability of software system analysis, whole software design and project management, strong practice and domain knowledge.

It is necessary for universities to establish training targets and patterns for software engineering talents with professional characteristics. To reach the goals, some important aspects, such as the construction of curriculum system, teaching material, teaching staff, practice training base, reform of teaching mode must be seriously considered.

2.5 Internationalization

2.5.1 Education Internationalization

With the development of high education of China, education internationalization has already become an important subject, and bilingual teaching and full English teaching are difficult points for education internationalization [9, 10]. It includes two sides: one is international education to domestic students, and the other is attracting, recruiting and training foreign students [11], which is very important to globalization education. But at present the attraction for foreign students in Chinese domestic universities is far behind first-class universities in the world [12], and an important constraint is the full English teaching ability.

2.5.2 The Full English Teaching Construction Scheme

The construction scheme of full English teaching concentrates in the following areas [13, 14]: teacher training, curriculum construction, international communication (foreign teachers hiring, delivery of international exchange and training for teachers, international visiting for domestic students, attracting international students), teaching platform construction (the text translation for existing platform, teaching secretary training, student status management internationalization) and teaching evaluation.

The evaluation of full English teaching has some similarity with Chinese teaching, while it also has distinctiveness. The evaluating of linguistic competence improvement and International Competitiveness is a full new topic.

2.6 Excellent Software Engineers Plan

The training of Excellent Engineers aimed at bringing up a large crowd of high quality engineering and technical talents who are more creative, economy and society development oriented [15–17]. "Excellence program" focuses on the following aspects: Objectives of engineering talents training, Enterprise management for students (including the self-organized simulated company learning, simulated company management and simulated company practice), centralized practice at the end of the semester, paying attention to foreign language learning, tip-top talents training, software engineer lecture and cultural forum.

"Software creates value, education refines soul". The utility of software engineering talents is one part of the strategy of revitalizing China through science and education, it conforms to the training requirements of the Excellent Engineers. As one of the national pilot software colleges, software college of Northeastern University did some solid work on practical software talents training and achieved good performance. Graduates from our college are warmly welcomed by employers. Based on the target of training Excellent Engineers, we will summarize the teaching and accumulate more valuable experience for Excellent Engineers training.

3 Conclusions

Based on the present situation and future trend of the information technology area, combined with the software engineering talents cultivation practice of software college of Northeastern University, this paper rethought software engineering specialty talents training, provided some common problems currently existed and put out some ideas for them. We believe that it is beneficial to improve future talents training, especially for the field of software engineering.

References

1. Wen, Z. (2007). Reform and exploration of higher vocational education curriculum. *Vocational Technical Education in China, 11*, 17–19.
2. http://today.banyuetan.org/jrt/120922/70953.shtml
3. http://www.ciotimes.com/infrastructure/sjk/59675.html

4. http://www.qikan.com.cn/Article/dxjx/dxjx201206/dxjx20120612-1.html
5. Free Online Course Materials and MIT Open Course Ware. http://ocw.mit.edu/index.htm
6. Zhang, Y. (2004). Transparence Computing: Concept, Architecture and Example, in ACTA Electronica SINICA, Vol. 32, No. 12A, Dec 2004.
7. Tao, W., & Fan, H. (2012). Research on cultivating mode for practical software talents. *Education and Vocation, 20,* 105–106.
8. Zhang, Y., & Tan, Z. (2011). Study on software talents cultivation in coal colleges. *Software Guide, 10*(12), 182–184.
9. Ma, Y., & Zhang, X. (2007). Present situation of bilingual teaching in China's university. *Journal of Peking University (Philosophy and Social Sciences), 5,* 66–67.
10. Jing, J., & Chen, Y. (2007). Analysis of current situation and practice of bilingual teaching in university. *Journal of Peking University (Philosophy and Social Sciences), 5,* 288–290.
11. Lu, X. (2006). Foreign students education and college internationalization process. *Journal of Linyi Normal College, 8,* 59–62.
12. Yu, T. (2006). Urgent need for strengthening foreign students education in university. *Journal of Cangzhou Normal College, 3,* 81–82.
13. Huo, Y., Wang, X., & Duan, X. (2008). Research on bilingual teaching for computer science. *Bilingual Teaching, 10,* 10–11.
14. Wu, J., & Xia, J. (2010). Cultivating scheme design for civil engineering (international class) under internationalization background. *Journal of Zhejiang Science and Technology College, 5,* 409–412.
15. National expert committee for programmatic accreditation of engineering education. National standards for programmatic accreditation of engineering education (Trial). Chinese Ministry of Education, 2007.
16. National expert committee for programmatic accreditation of engineering education. National working manuals for programmatic accreditation of engineering education. Chinese Ministry of Education, 2009.
17. Lin, J. (2010). Universal standard design of "excellent engineer education plan". *Research in higher education of engineering, 4,* 23–25.

An Initiative to Apply the Concept and Philosophy of Industry-Oriented Higher Education to Technician Level Software Programmes

Jenny Munnelly, Sharon Feeney, Bing Wu, Matt Hussey, Tom Duff, Pat O'Neill and Robert Burns

Abstract The series of CEISEE symposia has been largely focused on honours undergraduate and postgraduate software degree programmes. But the themes involved apply with equal emphasis and measure to programmes leading to ordinary level degrees or traditional technician level programmes, which normally have a heavy practical component. This chapter presents a recent initiative to present a month-long workshop on these themes at Dublin Institute of Technology (DIT) to some 25 teachers from a number of polytechnic colleges from the Beijing area and organised through the Institute for Vocational and Adult Education (IVEA) of the Beijing Academy of Educational Sciences and the Beijing Information Technology College (BITC).

Keywords Industry-oriented education · Higher education reform · Quality assurance · Software education in 3 year programmes · Technician education and training in software

J. Munnelly (✉) · S. Feeney · B. Wu · M. Hussey · T. Duff · P. O'Neill · R. Burns
Dublin Institute of Technology, Dublin, Ireland
e-mail: Jenny.Munnelly@dit.ie

S. Feeney
e-mail: sharon.feeney@dit.ie

B. Wu
e-mail: bing.wu@dit.ie

M. Hussey
e-mail: matthew.hussey15@gmail.com

T. Duff
e-mail: thomasjduff@gmail.com

P. O'Neill
e-mail: pjanoneill@yahoo.com

G. Motta and B. Wu (eds.), *Software Engineering Education for a Global E-Service Economy*, Progress in IS, DOI: 10.1007/978-3-319-04217-6_12,
© Springer International Publishing Switzerland 2014

1 Introduction

The series of symposia under the banner of the CEIS-SIOE/CEISIE/CEISEE over the past 8 years has been devoted to examining and enhancing the education and training of software graduates to enable them to effectively and efficiently enter the rapidly evolving globalised software industry. In pursuit of this aim a wide range of themes such as the nature of the modern software industry, the knowledge economy, the nature and impact of globalisation, the knowledge and skills needed in this industry, the role of the software industry in higher education (HE), the development of industry oriented software education with strong interactions between academic staff, students and industry, the development of appropriate curricula, programmes and teaching/learning approaches, the implementation of comprehensive quality assurance in these programmes, and many other related matters, have been explored. These themes have been further explored in a recent book [1].

The forces unleashed by globalisation exert unremitting pressure on students and graduates/workers as well as on academic institutions and countries to critically review, modernise and quality assure all levels and practices within the educational system. In the turbulent area of software education these forces for update and change are more pressing than in many other disciplines [2–4].

In general the emphasis within these symposia has been on programmes leading to undergraduate honours degrees and postgraduate taught and research degrees. It would probably be fair to say that the level of higher education just below the honours degree level, the level leading to an ordinary degree after a 3 year full-time programme, has not received a great deal of attention in these symposia. This has been a significant omission because there are many such software programmes producing thousands of recruits for the software industry, and the need for those workers to be prepared in knowledge, skills and competences for the requirements of the industry are every bit a pressing as for those with higher qualifications [5].

2 DIT Background

The Dublin Institute of Technology (DIT) was statutorily established as an autonomous institution by the DIT Act 1992 on 1 January 1993, constituted from the six higher education (HE) colleges with a history since 1887 of providing applied and higher vocational education and training programmes mainly in areas of science, technology and business. From the 1950s the colleges offered full-time programmes to prepare students for the examinations of professional bodies. From the mid-1960s, the colleges pioneered the development in Ireland of 3 year full-time technician education and training programmes, an initiative that was a key factor in subsequent national economic development. Through a partnership agreement with the University of Dublin (Trinity College, TCD) initiated in 1975, the higher diploma programmes of the colleges were recognised by TCD and their graduates were awarded honours degrees of the University. After a systematic institutional audit of DIT's quality assurance procedures and their effectiveness by the Higher Education Authority (HEA) during 1995/1996, degree-awarding powers to the highest postgraduate level were granted to DIT from 1998 [6].

With a quality-assured industry-oriented ethos and a strong commitment to the ladders of opportunity—clearly signposted possible paths for students to progress from lower level programmes to the highest level—the DIT educational model has proven robust, popular and nationally advantageous for some generations 7. The model has also attracted attention from China and other countries in the throes of development. Early in 2012 an approach was made to DIT by the Research Institute for Vocational and Adult Education (IVEA) of the Beijing Academy of Educational Sciences with regard to a training workshop for software lecturers/teachers in polytechnic colleges on the DIT educational model.

3 The Research Institute for Vocational and Adult Education in Beijing

The IVEA was established in 2000 to provide policy advice and guidance on best practice in professional and vocational education, and on issues such as curriculum design and organisation, teaching methods, evaluation, quality assurance, and the use of IT, particularly to polytechnic colleges in the Beijing region. Over the last 4 years the IVEA organised a series of training workshops in institutions outside China for groups of about 20 teachers/lecturers from these colleges to study and absorb the lessons of a range of educational models with an emphasis on information technology and the software industry.

The approach to DIT was a continuation of this series of workshops to learn of best international practice in 3 year vocational and professional programmes. Following discussions the IVEA arranged a Training Agreement between DIT and the Beijing Information Technology College (BITC) for a month-long training workshop for 25 teachers/lecturers from BITC and other polytechnic colleges in Beijing to be held in October 2012.

4 Programme of the BITC Workshop

There were two main modules in this training workshop, respectively on teaching/learning model for software education and on mobile software (App) development.

4.1 Module on DIT Teaching/Learning Model for Software Education

This module consisted of some 40 h of lectures distributed over the full 4 weeks of the programme. The themes covered in some detail were the following:

- an overview of the DIT education ethos, system and practice, and its place in Irish higher education
- the implementation of DIT's industry orientation to higher education
- a general introduction to academic quality assurance

  - programme design and development
  - the programme document
  - year/semester/module curriculum structure and integration,
  - module development, learning outcomes and testing for them
  - integration of modules, industry placement issues
  - teaching and learning approaches, matching to modules
  - industry placement issues
  - final year projects
  - assessments and examinations, process management, preparation, confidentiality, communication with academic and industrial external examiners, examination boards
  - programme committee
  - chairperson, class mentors, class representative system
  - periodic radical reviews of each programme
  - institutional reviews by external authorities with academic and industrial expertise.

As a final assessment of the module, the participants, working in groups of 3 or 4, were required to outline the design of an App to implement a quality assurance process suitable for their own college. At the end of the workshop, each group then collectively presented their project to the class as a whole and to the full group of workshop lecturers.

4.2 Module on Mobile Software (App) Development

This module consisted of 30 h lectures with supervised laboratory work spread over the month as well as some 30 h of self-study/laboratory work.

The aim was for participants to receive first-hand knowledge and practical skills from an educational model in Irish IT education. This included the key element of a taught technical module to enable participants to observe and study specific teaching methods in a core module. Issues addressed included module development and teaching mechanisms including curriculum design and the incorporation of emerging technologies and their applications in an academic module.

The module provided an introduction to the skills and techniques required to develop software that runs on a mobile device. It was practical in nature, with the emphasis on creating working software that could be executed on an emulator or deployed on a mobile device.

The module descriptor outlined the detailed aims, learning outcomes, learning and teaching methods, content and assessment methods of the module. The module aimed to provide a thorough introduction to the required skills and an understanding of the constraints of mobile development. It also aimed to illustrate how technologies can be used to develop full applications appropriate to smartphones, while also ensuring that students would be able to use the technologies they learned in a business and academic context. On completion of the module the learner would be able to design and develop full mobile applications through the technologies and content delivered using the tools taught in the module.

The content of the module focused on the use of the Android framework, a Java-based framework, and therefore familiarity with the Java programming language was a fundamental prerequisite. Theoretical areas including the architecture of the Android framework and details of the Dalvik Virtual Machine formed the basis of how the applications run. The majority of the content was practical in nature, building the development skills required to produce working Android applications. Areas covered include the basic components used to build applications, designing and building user interfaces (screens), techniques used to move from screen to screen, storing and reading information on mobile devices, playing music/video and interacting with the hardware on the device, such as capturing images using the camera.

Topics were explained in detail through slides, discussion and live examples in lectures. Participants completed relevant problem solving exercises in practical sessions using the lecture notes and examples while being further facilitated by the lecturer.

Exercises and assignments were given throughout the module for completion in the self-directed learning hours as formative assessments. Solutions to these assignments were discussed in class to enable participants to further develop their understanding. A larger project to develop a full mobile application using all elements of the module was set for completion by the participants, working in groups, at the end of the module. Each then gave a presentation demonstrating their application and describing the design and implementation of their working software. Each demonstration, presentation and project report was assessed and feedback on them provided by the academic team.

This module contributed in three key areas. Firstly, it illustrated a concrete example of the quality assurance processes that the participants had studied in the other module. It showed how a real world module is put together and documented using those processes. Secondly, it enabled the participants to experience the delivery of a technical module demonstrating teaching and learning methods. It also addressed the key issue of how assignments are designed and assessed, and how students can build on class work for practical assessments. Finally, it provided an opportunity for participants to experience the learning outcomes of the module, proving the benefits of providing industry relevant skills.

4.3 Industry-Orientation

During the workshop, emphasis was placed on illustrating the collaboration of DIT with industry in the provision of relevant academic programmes. DIT collaborates with organisations across many sectors to ensure that its programmes deliver the skills required by students to thrive in the workplace. One such collaboration is the MSc Applied Software Technology delivered by DIT and supported by ICT Ireland Skillnets and Ericsson. This is a combined initiative to produce work-ready graduates who are employed by Ericsson upon satisfactory completion of the academic programme. All the relevant skills are taught on the programme, as specified by the industry collaborator, Ericsson. The students then emerge with the required skillset and qualification relevant to the IT industry in Ireland. These graduates provide a pipeline of employees for Ericsson, enabling them continue to produce world leading technology in the telecommunications industry. This training workshop included a site visit to Ericsson in Athlone for a presentation from the company on how industry and academic collaboration is vital to ensuring graduates meet industry requirements.

A number of other sessions were also presented by guest speakers from industry (Datalex, Microsoft European Development Centre and Enterprise Ireland) on the following topics:

- knowing the requirements of industry
- strategic planning and the development of the Irish ICT industry and higher education
- introductions to the speakers' companies.

4.4 Review and Feedback Session

The workshop ended with a feedback session in which the lecturers provided evaluations and comments on the assessments and the participants offered feedback on the quality of their experience of the workshop, and the value to them of the subjects dealt with therein. The general impression was of considerable learning that could and would be applied to enhance the programmes and student learning in the home institutions of the participants.

All the participants successfully passed the assessments and a DIT continuing professional development (CPD) certificate in Internationalised Education in Technology Management, Innovation and Software Product Development was awarded to each.

5 Summary

The participating lecturers/teachers from the polytechnic colleges took a firm grasp of the relevance and importance to their teaching of the ideas and processes imparted to them in the workshop. They departed determined to strive to apply the lessons to the students in their colleges, as stated by the Chinese Counsellor from Chinese Embassy to Ireland at the award ceremony of the workshop that the Chinese students '...all play important roles in their respective colleges, I do believe they will spread the knowledge learned here and will greatly promote the development of the Chinese vocational education as well as contribute a lot in promoting educational exchanges and cooperation between China and Ireland'.

A follow-on review session has been scheduled by the IVEA, to be organised by the BITC in Beijing in May 2013. The DIT academic team will travel to Beijing to review and assess the progress in implementing the concepts and processes learned in the workshop by each participating lecturer/teacher since the workshop in October 2012 and to provide further feedback.

The final report on the training workshop to the Beijing Education Authority, produced by the leaders of the BITC group stated that 'with the research and experience of the vocational education system in Ireland, the horizons of our views on higher level vocational education have been broadened. The contents of this training programme were quite rich and included curriculum design and development, teaching methods and design of lecture series, education quality assurance ethos and system, cooperation between DIT and enterprises, industry visits, learning a cutting-edge technology, and experiencing DIT's learning and teaching methods. All of these activities have enabled us to come into contact with new material, broadening our horizons, enriching and equipping us with new learning and teaching perspectives to attain a higher level vocational education.'

To sum up, this training mission was a great success and should be further developed and implemented so as to enhance the industry-oriented higher education programmes in the polytechnic colleges to provide internationalised education in technology management, innovation and software product development.

References

1. Hussey, M., et al. (Eds.). (2011). *Software industry-oriented education practices and curriculum development: Experiences and lessons*. Hershey: IGI Global.
2. Friedman, T. L. (2005). *The world is flat: A brief history of the twenty-first century, Farrar*. New York: Straus & Giroux.
3. Lawless, D. (2007). Bridging the knowledge gap: Educating computer science graduates to work in a knowledge-based society. In *Proceedings of the International Technology, Education and Development Conference*, Valencia.

4. Carroll, D., et al. (2006). Stakeholders in the quality process of software engineering education. In *Proceedings of 2nd China Europe International Symposium on Software Industry-Oriented Education*, Harbin.
5. Forfás. (2007). *The fifth report of the expert group on future skills needs, tomorrow's skills needs: Towards a national skills strategy*, Dublin.
6. Duff, T., et al. (2000). *The story of the Dublin Institute of Technology*. Dublin: Blackhall.
7. Duff, T., et al. (2000). *Academic quality assurance in Irish higher education: Elements of a handbook*. Dublin: Blackhall.

From the Rise of CDIO (Conceive, Design, Implement and Operate) Process and "Modern Apprenticeship" to Exam the Direction of Reforming the Vocational Education in China

MinYing Xu

Abstract It is necessary to reform the higher vocational education according to the needs of social development, positing the students in the center of our concern, taking the path of integrating education and practices, and aiming at upgrading the overall ability of the students. Given the fruits of the reform of the International Higher Engineering Education (CDIO), this research suggests that to bringing in a Modern Apprenticeship would be a promotion of substantive reform in higher vocational education.

Keywords Reform of higher vocational education · Engineering education · Modern apprenticeship · CDIO

1 The Development of Higher Vocational Education in China

Industrial development has shifted higher vocational education from enterprises to higher level education institutes. The content and methods of education have gradually been transformed from empirical and practical experiences in workplace reality to theoretical and simulative settings in classrooms. The way and the ability of obtaining knowledge have changed to be direct, discrete, and generalized, rather than were indirect, continuous, and specialized. Educators of vocational skills were craft-masters, who were directly capable of putting the skills to use, developing new skills, and directly benefited from the techniques. Now the educators have become lecturers, who are nonusers of the techniques and knowledge and thus indirectly related to the skills. Apprentices and students learn differently. Apprentices start

M. Xu (✉)
Beijing Information Technology College, Bejing, China
e-mail: Xumy@bitc.edu.cn

G. Motta and B. Wu (eds.), *Software Engineering Education for a Global E-Service Economy*, Progress in IS, DOI: 10.1007/978-3-319-04217-6_13,   109
© Springer International Publishing Switzerland 2014

from the workplace settings where they working on particular but having the whole system in mind. On the other hand, students learn in classrooms where they practice outside the workplace reality and thus having little conscience of the whole system when they are exposed to particular yet abstract piece of knowledge.

Higher vocational education left workshops and entered into High Education Institutes; this is an unsurprising consequence of large-scale industrial development. As a wave of the age, this shift has been a powerful motor to propel further industrial change. It is necessary to meet large-scale industry's demands by transforming higher vocational education from craftsmanship to specialized education. Having been established as dependent disciplines, vocational education works along with technique development and thrive as the time's trend.

2 Approaches to Learning

2.1 The Emergence of the Modern Apprenticeship: A Return

As time changes, one salient feature of the modern science and technology is that the one dominant position of hardware was given into software, which has become the soul of technology. Production line has been gradually replaced by job islands and positions in project teams. Such occupational changes have changed work organizations.

Workers who are bounded to positions become parts of the machine, and they can be trained for adjusting mechanical parts. However, while working in a project team, under a more flexible work system environment, with complex technology, or exploring innovations and approaching divergent goals, workers begin to return to their human nature—in other words, to intellectual actions. In terms of technology development, it is a return to systematic, professional, and creative features of new technology.

Bringing human values back to work must have an impact on education. As a result, "Modern Apprenticeship" (e.g. UK's NVQ in 1990s and TAFE in Australia TAFE [1]. Germany's dual system actually counts as another example.) has emerged. Modern Apprenticeship in vocational education combines formal academic education and craftsmanship together. It has some key characteristics. Firstly, students are engaged in industrial reality while learning, which enhances understanding of the whole system of production and internalizes professional conscience in a professional environment. Secondly, objective and paths of personal development are very clear. Thirdly, students can easily relate particular work procedures to the whole system by practicing a particular procedure with a big picture. Fourthly, learning is complete, and this combines personal ability, social competence, technical competence, corporate culture, linking knowledge and ability into an organic whole rather than dry preaching. Fifthly, knowledge is transferred into practice, which produces skills of potential to further develop. Sixthly, mistakes and failures become meaningful learning process which fosters ability of solution exploration. All of the above comply with theories of effective learning.

2.2 Higher Education: CDIO Engineering Education Model

For higher education in the engineering disciplines, CDIO is currently an important academic progress. CDIO is the abbreviation of Conceive, Design, Implement and Operate. By experiencing the life cycle from product development to product implementation, students are allowed to learn engineering in an active and engaged way in which knowledge from different courses are connected organically. The CDIO's syllabus is divided into four levels—basic knowledge on engineering, personal ability, teamwork, and systematic ability of engineering. Students are required to meet requirements on all four levels. The CDIO system develops 12 standards to cultivate ability, implement the syllabus, and evaluate results [2].

So far, there have been many world-renowned universities, which have joined the CDIO organization. The students who are trained by CDIO mode are popular with enterprises and general society. In recent years, CDIO engineering education model has been implemented by a number of universities in China, which has been proven to be effective. Shantou University took the first step in adopting the CDIO in vocational education. With the support and guidance from the Department of Higher Education of the Ministry of Education, CDIO later was expansively piloted by many universities appointed as experimental spots and also adopted by other universities which were not experimental spots. CDIO has helped those universities to make fruitful progress in reforming vocational education. Diffusion of CDIO in China settled the ground for implementing "the Project of Cultivating Excellent Engineers" in China and also positively promoted that project and guaranteed the quality in implementing this project [3, 4].

2.3 Modern Apprenticeship and CDIO for Higher Vocational Education in Higher Education

Many factors restrict the development of vocational education in China. One main question is how to promote vocational education for the industry and closely integrate education with the actual production. With the further development of industrialization and information technology, simple operation has been replaced by systematic and coordinative work. One dimensional education in schools must be supplemented by enterprises. For the reform of higher vocational education, three aspects of CDIO mode and Modern Apprenticeship can be drawn:

1. *Setting the goal of higher vocational education*

   Before designing and describing the goal of a vocational education, there must be a clear picture of abilities required by the target industry. This picture must be vivid enough to prepare students to fully understand the direction of their development, their current level, and the distance from the final goal. Lecturers should cite this picture frequently when guiding the students. This picture works as a map and a ruler to measure students' growth (CDIO refers to it as the introduction to engineering which holds the key to provoke students' interest in learning). But who should draw this picture? Here lies the value of cooperation between the industry and schools. With the industry's deep involvement, this picture will be drawn well and receive prompt updates.

2. *Elements of the methodology of higher vocational education*

   (a) The learning environment. A learning environment for systematic vocational development is a key to the campus culture. A good campus culture should make people sense the spirits of professionalism, creativity, and advocacy of technology.

   (b) Content of learning. Content of learning must reflect the need of a vocation rather than of a discipline. Comprehensive ability should be integrated into each course, rather than fragmented by each course. The curriculum design should connected courses into a dynamic system with dense connections between each other.

   (c) Learning method. From independent study, project-based learning, to team based learning, as long as it can help to develop vocational ability, the method should be absorbed as a part the learning solutions. Exam-oriented learning is the one that should be abandoned.

3. *The role of vocational education lecturers*

   Higher vocational education is an organic part of production in reality, and thus the lecturers for vocational education must have the ability to cope with industrial realities.

   (a) Lecturers should be from the industry. Regardless of the teaching tasks, lecturers should have a clear view of the target industry's occupational components, professional abilities, and engineering system. Students need a lecturer who is 'know-all' about the target industry.

   (b) Lecturers should also have teaching expertise and be equipped with methodology of teaching and learning. In the age of rapid information exchanges, students grow up with internet which allows them to access information in a bidirectional way. When they are receiving information, they also desire to have control over their own learning progress and study contents. Unidirectional lecturing cannot function effectively any more.

   (c) The lecturer should set up an example for the students. The students desire a lecturer of charisma. Lecturers with an extensive practical knowledge, offering guidance for career choice, or with skillful practical ability always gain popularity among students. This proves that students are motivated by objectives of learning. Lecturers are not only teaching in lectures, but also teaching through settling up role models for students.

3 The Successful Case of Beijing Information Technology College

3.1 Setting the Goal of Vocational Education by College-Enterprise Cooperation

Each major in BITC has a "committee of college-enterprise cooperation". Taking the major of software technology as an example, the committee is constituted with software engineer, testing engineer, system analysts, system architect, project manager, and professor and associate professor from the school. The map of vocational ability and skills for software technology is determined by this committee.

3.2 Beixin Software Park: A Training Base of College-Enterprise Cooperation

BITC founded "Beixin Software Park" in 2008 as a practical training base. The park includes the software development zone, digital art creation zone, embedded software development zone, new technique experiment zone, computer science research center, and administration area for college-enterprise cooperation, and etc., which realizes the model of 'industry within school'. Enterprises which used to be and now are still based in the park are: Bluewave Internet Technology, Hanmark Tech, Beijing Kuka Animation, Beijing Ouleba High-tech, Mingdeli High-tech, Juskin, and Sinosys. BITC offers these enterprises rent discount and other benefits; these enterprises in turn offered students of BITC "projects" for practical training and appoint engineers as project managers.

3.3 Project Management in Practical Training as a Form of Modern Apprenticeship and CDIO Education Model

Project-based practical training is a way to transfer project management in enterprises into project-based teaching around which practical training is carried out. It has the following characteristics:

1. Through school-enterprise cooperation, project is suggested by enterprises.
2. Engineers from enterprises and lecturers from the school work together as project managers for the practical training project.

3. Practical training in the industrial reality reveals the whole process of vocational involvement, including recruitment, orientation, forming project team, distribution of tasks, control of production process, assessment of performance, and grading. Students participate in the whole project process according to the CDIO education model.

3.4 The Practical Effects of Project-Based Training

1. Ability enhancement: Since 2008, senior students of the majors of software technology, embedded practical technology, information management, internet technology, internet system management, animation, advertisement design and production, electronic business and etc. have participated in project-based practical training. Through completing each real project, students practice the newest technology, understand norms for engineering, accumulate experiences, obtain professional skills, which in all levels up the overall quality of students' ability. The according level-up of competition is measured by the proportion in graduates who get jobs that match their major in vocational education. This figure has increased from 50 to 80 % after the implementation of project-based training with principles of modern apprenticeship and CDIO education model.
2. Expansion of the management system of project-based practical training: BITC's computer science research center independently created "the management system of project-based practical training", which is a platform of practical training management designed according to the principles of project management in enterprises. This system can realize the process management from project initiation to project assessment. It can also set up evaluation programs, criteria, and the comprehensive evaluation system. Besides of BITC, this system has been adopted or intended to adopt by Beijing Union University and higher vocational schools in Xinjiang.

3.5 Exploration of Innovative Education Projected Based on CDIO Education Model

In 2012, BITC and Dublin Institute of Technology (DIT) signed agreement on cooperation of education. In September of 2012, BITC assigned a delegate to DIT and examined DIT's business incubator for its graduates which was a highly inspiring trip. In 2013, BITC will sign another agreement with Beijing Peony Incubator Company (Peony) to build a branch of Peony in Beixin Software Park and found a foundation for innovation in technology created by college students.

By now, the office building for Peony has been completed and campaign to promote innovative education is undergoing. In July of 2013, it is expected to welcome the first innovations of college students to enter the incubator.

4 Conclusions

"Higher vocational education should cut into the reform from the combination of industry and school and explore teaching models of integration of industry and school, task driven learning, project-based direction of teaching, and practices in real industrial positions, which all enhance students' ability. From the cooperation with the schools, enterprises can also share resources of the school, while participating reform in education and generate innovations in education. Higher vocational education must closely relate to industries, integrate with industries, and actively involve in building practical training bases within schools, which receive place and management from the schools, while equipments, techniques, and technicians from enterprises, carrying out practical training around the enterprise's projects [5]."

In the reform to realize integration between industry and schools, CDIO model and modern apprenticeship have shown successful practices in setting up educational goals, educational ideals, educational patterns, learning environments, and standards of lecturers. They are important models for our reform in vocational education.

References

1. Rui, X. (2008). *The Traditional Apprenticeship Comparative Study of Modern Apprenticeship, Theory of Consumer Guide, Phase IV.*
2. Crawley, E. (2009). *Rethinking Engineering Education: The CDIO Approach.* Chinese translation by Peihua, Gu. Higher Education Press.
3. Gu, P., Bao, N., Kang, Q., Lu, X., Xiong, G., Lin, P., & Chen, Y. (2012). *Gaodeng Gongcheng Jiaoyu Yanjiu* (Research on Higher Education of Engineering).
4. Chinese Ministry of Education. (2011). *Suggestions on Implementation of Project of Cultivating Excellent Engineers.*
5. Ministry of Education. (2006). *Suggestions on Comprehensive Improvement of the Quality of Higher Vocational Education.*

Part III
Curricula for Software Engineering Education

To Cultivate Engineering Leadership of Excellent Undergraduate Students in HIT-NPSS

Dong Li, Guo-Xiang Fan, Pei-Jun Ma and Xiao-Fei Xu

Abstract The development of software engineering needs not only excellent software engineers, but also outstanding engineering leaders. In the past 90 years, Harbin Institute of Technology (HIT) has graduated a lot of outstanding engineering leaders. Based on the successful environment and experiences, in December 2012 HIT launched a program for candidate engineering leader cultivation (CELECA), and National Pilot School of Software (NPSS) became one of experimental schools. The background of the CELECA program is introduced at first, and then the proposal of CELECA in NPSS is presented. Finally, the executive plan and progress is described.

Keywords Engineering leadership · Project-based learning · Software engineering education · Industry-oriented education

1 Introduction

In the past 60 years, there has been a significant development in software engineering domain. The development benefited from not only a lot of excellent software engineers, but also from outstanding engineering leaders, as Frederick P. Brooks of IBM, Bill Gates of Microsoft, and Linus Torvalds. So, the importance of cultivation of engineering leaders is recognized by some universities. The MIT in U.S.A. piloted the Gordon Engineering Leadership Program from the fall semester of 2007 [1].

D. Li (✉) · G.-X. Fan · P.-J. Ma · X.-F. Xu
School of Software, Harbin Institute of Technology, Harbin, China
e-mail: lee@hit.edu.cn

P.-J. Ma
e-mail: ma@hit.edu.cn

X.-F. Xu
e-mail: xiaofei@hit.edu.cn

G. Motta and B. Wu (eds.), *Software Engineering Education for a Global E-Service Economy*, Progress in IS, DOI: 10.1007/978-3-319-04217-6_14,
© Springer International Publishing Switzerland 2014

In the past 90 years, Harbin Institute of Technology (HIT) has cultivated a large number of high quality engineers. Therefore, the HIT was regarded as the Cradle of Engineers. Some of them became outstanding engineering leaders, such as Sun Jiadong, the father of Chinese satellite, Xu Dazhe, the chief leader of experimental team of Chinese Manned spacecraft, Ma Xingrui, the CEO of China Aerospace Science and Technology Corporation (CASC), Gao Qunyao, the former CEO of Autodesk (China) Co. Ltd.

Since 2000, HIT has made a great progress in the cultivation of high quality engineers. For example, the student team from HIT won the champion of 2009 Asia-Pacific Broadcast Unit Robot Contest (ABU-ROBOCON). The platform technique of advanced micro satellite was chosen as one of top10 High-tech progress made by Chinese universities in 2012 by the Ministry of Education of China, that were developed by faculty staff and graduate students of HIT.

Based on the environment and experiences in successful cultivation of excellent engineers, in December of 2012 HIT launched a program for candidate engineering leader cultivation (CELECA), to meet the developing requirement of IT industry in China, and to achieve the HIT's goal to become a first class university in the world. 9 schools in HIT were selected to be experimental schools of CELECA.

Founded in 2000, the HIT National Pilot School of Software (HIT-NPSS) has been insisting the idea of "Internationalization, Industrialization, High-quality, High-speed", has established an educational environment of software engineering talents based on the cooperation with IT companies, that includes faculty staff with industrial feature, curriculum that emphasis industrial skills, industrial teaching approach such as Project-Based Learning(PjBL), 4-weeks' enterprise on-site training, One-year enterprise internship, Entrepreneur Forum, Student Clubs of software techniques, etc. [2].

The graduates of HIT-NPSS were warmly welcomed by the IT companies, because they could create values for their bosses from the first day they entered the companies without any training overhead. According to the statistics, more than 90 % of HIT-NPSS graduates were employed by international enterprises, national fortune 500, research institutes and IT companies. More than 50 % of graduates were employed by internship base companies or their partner companies [3].

In 2010, the program of software engineering in the HIT-NPSS was selected to be experimental program of excellent engineer cultivation plan by the Ministry of Education (MOE) of China. In 2011, Lei Yong and Wang Shibo were granted the "Top 10 outstanding MSEs" and "Top 10 outstanding bachelors of SE" respectively in the tenth anniversary of NPSS by the MOE. Based on these achievements, the HIT-NPSS became one of experimental schools of CELECA.

2 The Scheme and Curriculum of CELECA in HIT-NPSS

Based on the cooperation with IT companies, there are two significant features of CELECA. One is that the senior managers or senior engineers of IT companies will take part in cultivating younger talents, and personally act as advisors of students in CELECA program. And the other is that the students will be involved in the high level managing activities of IT companies, as assistants of senior managers or senior engineers. The selected IT companies, to which the CELECA students enter as intern, are outstanding IT companies in China, as IBM China Company Ltd., ChinaSoft International Ltd., Neusoft Group Ltd. These companies will be authorized as "The CELECA base of HIT-NPSS".

The curriculum of CELECA in NPSS is based on the normal of bachelor curriculum of Software Engineering, but adds extra courses and enhanced training, aiming to promote students' engineering leadership. In normal curriculum, the students' world outlook, humanistic quality, basic knowledge of advanced mathematics and nature science are built by general education. The professional knowledge, with the abilities of software engineering and innovation are cultivated in a phase of professional education. The abilities of problem-solving, communication and demonstration are cultivated via the experience of project practices or PjBL [4].

The extra courses of the CELECA curriculum include Management foundations and case studies, Engineering leadership and communication, Project Management, Organizational behavior and team construction, etc.

The project practices of normal curriculum are enhanced with an emphasis on engineering leadership. The students in CELECA program are asked to act as the leader of a project team, and go through the whole process of a project, from selection of project, application for funding, system design, implementation and deployment. During the process, the team would past proposal review, midterm progress check-up, on-site inspection.

3 The Roadmap of CELECA in HIT-NPSS

The program of CELECA starts from spring semester of third year, and will last until the students get their MSE degree. Figure 1 depicts the program of CELECA in HIT-NPSS.

In the spring semester of third year, the students in CELECA will take extra courses to form the base of engineering leadership, and implement at least one IT project to cultivate their preliminary engineering leadership. The students must pass the examination of the courses or the final check of their projects. Otherwise they would asked to exit the CELECA. In the fourth year, i.e. the last year of bachelor program, the students in CELECA would enter IT companies as intern, take part in real projects, and finish their dissertations.

A double-adviser policy is carried out in HIT-NPSS: a student should have two advisers for his dissertation, one faculty teacher in campus, and one IT engineer in the company. The company advisers will instruct students on how to design and implement a software system; campus advisers appraise the difficulty and workload of the development, and they assess whether it matches the requirements of

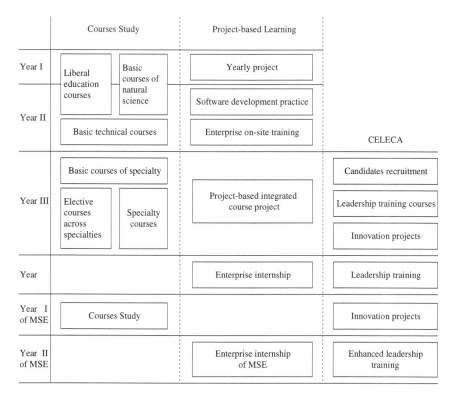

	Courses Study	Project-based Learning	
Year I	Liberal education courses / Basic courses of natural science	Yearly project	
Year II		Software development practice	
	Basic technical courses	Enterprise on-site training	CELECA
Year III	Basic courses of specialty	Project-based integrated course project	Candidates recruitment
	Elective courses across specialties / Specialty courses		Leadership training courses
			Innovation projects
Year		Enterprise internship	Leadership training
Year I of MSE	Courses Study		Innovation projects
Year II of MSE		Enterprise internship of MSE	Enhanced leadership training

Fig. 1 Diagram of CELECA in HIT-NPSS

university dissertation, and instruct students on how to write their dissertations at the end of internship.

The students in CELECA have privileges to enter the CELECA bases of HIT-NPSS, that are well-known IT companies, and their candidate campus advisers are senior lecturers with strong background of R&D, their candidate company advisers must be high-level managers or senior engineers.

By the agreement with the CELECA bases of HIT-NPSS, the students in CELECA not only get the personally instruction or guidance from high-level managers or senior engineers, but also have opportunities to involve in the managing activities or project argumentation.

By such a training approach, the students in CELECA could learn a lot from their advisers beyond techniques. For example, the art of management, how to tradeoff in decision making, the culture of enterprise, team work and communication, career planning, strong willpower facing challenges, enterprising spirit, etc.

To ensure the quality of internship, NPSS carries out proposal review, midterm progress check-up, on-site inspection during the process of internship. If one student fails in one of above inspections, he would be asked to exit the CELECA.

At the end of internship, a basic engineering leadership of students in CELECA will be developed. They would go back to the campus to participate in dissertation defense. If they get their bachelor degree with score of B or above, they will be awarded additional honor certificates of CELECA for undergraduate students. After graduation, the students will continue to study in NPSS for MSE to fulfill the complete CELECA program.

Besides carrying out the normal curriculum, the students in CELECA would be asked to organize and lead a student team in the first year of MSE, to finish at least an innovative project under the guidance of their campus advisers.

In the second year, i.e. the last year of MSE program, the students in CELECA will enter the same IT companies that they entered in program of bachelor as intern, take part in real projects and finish their dissertations with same advisers. If they get their master degree with score of B or above, they will be awarded additional honor certificates of CELECA for graduate students.

4 The Recruitment of CELECA in HIT-NPSS

4.1 The Advantages and Application Condition of CELECA

The students in CELECA have priority to get the approval of innovation projects supported by HIT or MOE, to win a scholarship of HIT or MOE, and to be selected as an honor graduate. Once a student successfully completes the program of CELECA, he/she would be awarded an additional honor certificate of CELECA. The applicants must be in the top 20 % in the score ranking, i.e. excellent students. And they must have experiences that act as a team leader in the project practices or PjBL.

4.2 The Time and Approach to Recruitment

At the beginning of spring semester, a recruiting propaganda of CELECA would be hold for the junior student. In the propaganda, the advantages of CELECA, the application condition and approach to recruit would be announced. The applicants should hand in a career plan and participate in an interview for recruit. In the interview, the applicants would be asked to give a presentation and answer the questions of the interviewers. At the end of the interviews, the name list of candidates of CELECA will be announced. In the following week, the candidates and advisers will choose each other. At the end of this week, the choice would be done and results will be published. Then the program of CELECA can start.

5 Summary and Prospects

By the execution of CELECA, the students would become familiar to the businesses and cultures of the IT companies, for they had stayed in the same company nearly 3 years. In this way, the companies can find a leader of future with low overhead and little mistake, and the university will be proud of a distinguished alumnus in the future. So the CELECA is win–win. Nowadays, the scheme and curriculum of CELECA have made in NPSS. In following spring semester, not more than five students would be recruited as the first batch of CELECA. We are confident that the CELECA in HIT-NPSS would contribute to the development of the IT industry and improve the quality of higher education in HIT.

References

1. Crawley, E. F., & Bernard, M. (2007). Gordon—MIT Leadership Program: Developing engineering leaders of tomorrow. *MIT Faculty Newsletter. XX, I*(4), 6–7.
2. Xu, X. (2005). The approach and practice of software industry oriented education in China. *Journal of Harbin Institute of Technology, 12,* 1–3.
3. Liu, S., Ma, P., & Li, D. (2013). The Exploration and practice of gradually industrialization model in software engineering education—a factual instance of the excellent engineer plan of China. In *Proceeding of CSEE&T 2012* (pp. 23–31).
4. Li, D., Ma, P., & Liu, S. (2012). To cultivate outstanding software engineer based on project-based learning. *Computer Education, 10,* 23–27.

The Solutions to Strengthening the Construction of Computer Experimental Teaching Faculty

Chun He, Hang Lei, Qihua Wang and Xinyuan Gong

Abstract This chapter investigates the ability that should be possessed by students majoring in Computer Science. We analyze the procedure of experimental teaching and the obstacles encountered in the construction of the teaching faculty, and we discuss some measures to strengthen the development of experimental teaching.

Keywords Computer technology · Software engineering · Experimental teaching · Internship · Faculty

1 Introduction

The courses demand a wide range of abilities. The ability of students should encompass cognitive, practical, and innovation abilities:

- Cognitive ability includes the ability to comprehend a basic knowledge on computer software and hardware, to solve daily matters by using computers, and to comply with law and ethics in the information society.
- Practical ability includes the ability to acquire, analyze, and use information, to manage and use information by related software, to solve problems in professional field by technology.
- Innovation ability refers to the capability of taking advantage of computer technology to design and develop cross-field applications.

C. He (✉) · H. Lei · Q. Wang · X. Gong
School of Computer Science and Engineering, School of Information and Software Engineering, University of Electronic Science and Technology of China, Chengdu, China
e-mail: hechun@uestc.edu.cn

X. Gong
e-mail: gongxy@uestc.edu.cn

G. Motta and B. Wu (eds.), *Software Engineering Education for a Global E-Service Economy*, Progress in IS, DOI: 10.1007/978-3-319-04217-6_15,
© Springer International Publishing Switzerland 2014

Feng Boqin [1] identifies three levels of ability, namely (a) the acquisition of computer knowledge, (b) the use of computer technology, and (c) the creation process. Zhang Shiju [2] explains effective experimental teaching patterns, based on existing problems and required conditions. Hong Ying [3] proposes "one center, three combinations and five changes" as a guideline, through a network-based laboratory management platform, to implement experimental teaching on experimental time, experimental resources, experimental courses, experimental projects and experimental evaluation. Zhou Xuanchang [4] proposes hierarchical teaching contents and their corresponding experimental capacity-building programs; teachers can use different teaching methods and teaching evaluation systems according to the different levels of experimental teaching to cultivate students' experimental attitudes. Niu Honghui and Huang Yongcan [5] introduce the structure of a new experimental teaching system and describe the research and exploration of innovation from the perspective of experimental teaching, experimental system, course examination mode, demonstration center building, and construction of experimental teaching team. Further discussions have been developed on [6–11] problems and limits of experimental and practical teaching. Our purpose is to further expand our insight into computer experimental teaching.

The three levels of ability imply three levels in computer experimental teaching: acquisition of basic knowledge, verification of the acquired knowledge, and innovative construction of systems. Thus the experimental education of undergraduates students should integrate the courses of fundamental, verification and comprehensive innovative experiments. And experimental teaching should proceed from easy to difficult, from simple to complex thus ensuring students can master computer knowledge and technology. Also the experimental system should be systematic.

The three core elements for education are students, teachers and teaching management. In order to adapt students to the needs of society and enterprises, universities should develop cooperation with stakeholders, like societies, companies, collaborative enterprises, institutions for engineering certification, internship institutions, etc. By those means we can set the qualification and feedback systems. The process of such education is in Fig. 1. Accordingly, we can gradually implement practical and engineering-oriented industrialization.

In the process in Fig. 1, practical teaching and experiments and corporate training in campus and engineering practice are two closely-related sections; therefore, both play an important role. After acquiring some basic knowledge, practical teaching and experiments improve cognitive ability, meanwhile internships in campus enterprises and engineering practice enhances the ability to a higher, which is called practical and creative ability. Those two phase should lead the current system of higher education in China.

However, the current computer experimental teaching in colleges or universities has gone to a different way. On one side, it is easy to offer fundamental and verification experiments, while it is hard to offer comprehensive innovative experiments. On the other side, due to the rapid development of computer technology, the phenomenon of "learning while teaching" is becoming more and more

Fig. 1 The training process
of software talent oriented
industrialization

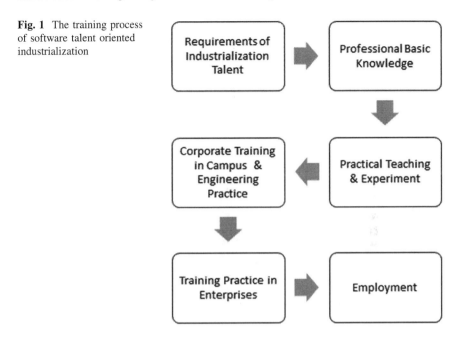

obvious. As a matter of fact, experimental teaching, if it is limited to a repetition of professional knowledge, causes students to lose interest. Training programs are lacking of complete experimental systems; those actually existing are divided into independent courses with little relationship. So is a bare supplement to the classroom teaching. Hence little attention has been paid to those courses by students and teachers. In short, level and effect of experimental teaching are related to teachers. To change the current situations, we have to start first from the faculty and systems.

2 The Analysis of Problems Emerging in Computer Experimental Teaching

2.1 The Infrastructure of Experimental Teaching Faculty

We have collected information on national experimental teaching demonstration centers. Statistics are in Figs. 2, 3 and 4. Letters A to J indicate, respectively, Peking University, Tsinghua University, Beijing University of Aeronautics and Astronautics, Harbin Institute of Technology, Tongji University, Southwest University, Hangzhou Dianzi University, Xi'an Jiaotong University, Lanzhou Jiaotong University and University of Electronic Science and Technology of China. The total number of the faculties for each university are A of 71, B of 66, C of 42, D of 84,

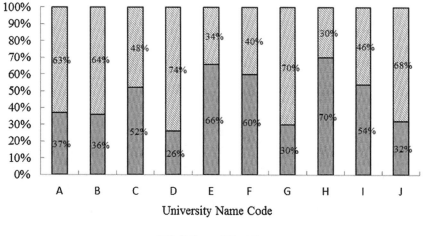

Fig. 2 Team structure

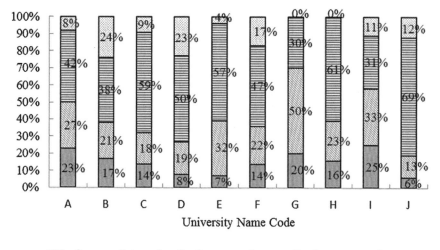

Fig. 3 Title composition of full time staff

E of 85, F of 82, G of 100, H of 46, I of 67 and J of 103 respectively. Figure 2 shows full time and the part time ratios for each university. Figure 3 indicates the composition of full time staff. Figure 4 represents the educational level of full time staff.

The ratio of full-time to part-time teachers in experimental teaching is approximately 1:1. Generally, full-time has lower degrees or titles than part-time

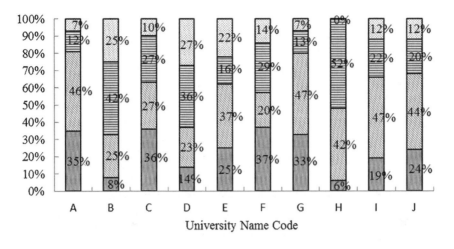

Fig. 4 Educational level of full time staff

staff, and part-time teachers have research background. So part-time experimental teachers are the most important part of teachers in experimental teaching. However, some part-time teachers are only registered to the posts but poorly assume their responsibilities, and even do not take duties at all. This lies in infrastructure of managing experimental faculties.

In colleges or universities, teachers, full-time researchers, administrative staffs and counselors are clearly classified. The duties, salaries and promotions of those jobs are regulated. By contrast, the job position of teachers in experimental teaching is unclear, since it does not belong to any specific level, e.g. either teacher, service or management. And the job is marginalized as a supplementary job to the teaching system, making it a closed system that no young teachers are willing to join.

2.2 The Incentive Mechanism for Experimental Teaching

The incentive mechanism for experimental teaching cannot keep up with the pace of increasing requirements of personnel training. Colleges or universities have systematic incentive policies on promotions of posts, ways of education and rewards for teachers and researchers, making expenditures on teaching or researching by teachers highly acknowledged and recognized, and thus teachers themselves are recognized mentally and materially as well. Conversely, the incentive mechanism for the faculty of experimental teaching is old-fashioned and cannot motivate teachers well.

2.3 The Position of Experimental Teachers in Universities

Teachers in experimental teaching don't have a clear path for personal development. While other teachers can be promoted as professors, excellent teachers loved by students, administrative staffs can also be promoted, teachers in experimental teaching mostly don't have a clear path for personal development, which is essentially disadvantageous in the development of personal career.

2.4 The Building Initiatives of Computer Professional Experimental Faculty

Teachers in experimental teaching have lower level of satisfaction and professional pride. And their values and achievements are not acknowledged and recognized equally due to mechanisms, policies, and the current situations of faculties in experimental teaching. It's not going well for those teachers personally or as a group in development.

3 Proposed Approaches to Construct the Computer Experimental Faculty Infrastructure

Once problems occurred in the faculties of experimental teaching, most of time, they are universal, lasting and difficult to solve. The linchpin to solving those problems lies in the highly attention by people in every related area. To the faculties in experimental teaching, the solution is to subdivide the posts, to invent some new systems for those teachers, and to eliminate the gaps between course teachers and teachers in experimental teaching, and also we should arrange teaching resources more rationally for education, and classify experimental teaching and related teachers to the system of education. By doing so, it would be a beneficial exploration to solve those problems.

At first, we should proceed with the requirements for faculties in experimental teaching in the education system, forming a general structure beneficial to the construction of the faculty of experimental teaching. Firstly, we should be aware that teachers in experimental teaching are part of the overall faculties. According to the requirements in the plan of education and curriculum, experimental teaching is an important section, so faculties in experimental teaching should be the important part of the teaching faculty, and should be given the correct recognition. Secondly, we should subdivide the experimental teaching according to the requirements in the plan of education and curriculum, and get to know different requirements for different levels and types of experimental teaching, forming the structure of a team including the experimental teaching leader + the experimental teaching backbone + the experimental teaching assistant, and the experimental managers.

The post of the experimental teaching leader should be held by professors in different fields, whose duty is to plan systematically for the faculty and the direction of teaching, including the experimental teaching, the setup of related courses, arrangements of the faculty, job rating, feedback in teaching, etc. thus to make it a systematic and closed process.

The post of the experimental teaching backbone should be held by doctors or Mid/Senior level job titles. They should independently accomplish the plans made by the experimental teaching leader, and make some feedback and suggestions in teaching.

The post of the experimental teaching assistant should be held by teachers who are new to teaching. They have little experience in teaching and are not so familiar with the education plans, and should get to know more about core requirements in education. They should teach by assisting teaching backbones, do tasks such as answer questions, instructing, correcting homework, participating in research or reforms. According to the training, they will become a teaching backbone, even the teaching leader later. Teachers other than the three types listed above should be separated out of the faculty, and should be put into posts of experiment management for service.

Second, we should work hard to construct the team of the experimental teaching leader. The linchpin to the construction of the experimental teaching faculty is the leading teachers. We can set up one or two experimental teaching leaders in every major by making attractive policies or according to some regulations in education. Those leading teachers should be the teaching leaders or the academic leaders in this major, whose duty mainly lies in the planning of experimental teaching systems, the design of courses in experimental teaching and some research and reforms in related areas and the deploy of the faculty.

Third, we should do more in the construction of backbone teaching teams. At present colleges or universities are not lacking in teachers. What they lack are teachers in experimental teaching. Thus we should regard and reward course teaching and experimental teaching equally. And we should remove differences in course teaching and experimental teaching, making excellent teachers willing to devote themselves to experimental teaching. And we ought to provide more support to research and reforms in experimental teaching, not only just spend money on experimental facilities. So that we can make more and more teachers regain the value, satisfaction and pride in experimental teaching.

Finally, we should regulate the duties of the administrative staff in experimental teaching, ensuring them working willingly, and thus to optimize the overall level of the faculty in experimental teaching and to improve the level to ensure the experimental teaching going well.

References

1. Feng, B. (2008, October). Deepening computer experiment teaching system reform to improve students' computer practice ability (Chinese), the 4th forum on the computer courses of university.
2. Zhang, S. (2008, May). Optimization of experimental teaching in electronic commerce. In *2008 International Conference on Computer Science and Software Engineering* (pp. 466–469). IEEE.
3. Hong, Y. (2009, March). Research on the Open Experimental Teaching Mode for Computer Major. In *IFCSTA'09. International Forum on Computer Science-Technology and Applications* (Vol. 3, pp. 380–382). IEEE.
4. Zhou, X. (2010, March). Reform and research on experimental teaching for high frequency electronic circuit. In *2010 International Conference on E-Health Networking, Digital Ecosystems and Technologies* (Vol. 2, pp. 168–170). IEEE.
5. Honghui, N., & Yongcan, H. (2010, February). Innovation of experimental teaching system base on ability cultivation. In *2010 International Conference on Future Information Technology and Management Engineering* (Vol. 2, pp. 451–454). IEEE.
6. Gu, M., Yao, X., & Qiu, M. (2010, February). Researches on the Innovation of Experimental and Practical Teaching on Environmental Science. In *2010 Second International Workshop on Education Technology and Computer Science* (Vol. 2, pp. 627–629). IEEE.
7. Zhou, S. (2011, October). Research report on Computer experimental teaching demonstration center (Chinese). The 1st forum on the computer experimental teaching.
8. Honghui, N. (2010, April). Research on public experimental teaching in computer application course reform. In *Second International Conference on Multimedia and Information Technology* (Vol. 1, pp. 119–121). IEEE.
9. Jiali, X., & Xia, S. (2012, July). Discussion and application in the mode of the "Teaching-studying-practicing" in computer basic teaching. In *7th International Conference on Computer Science & Education* (pp. 1780–1781). IEEE.
10. Xu, Z., Luo, C., & Zhang, Y. (2012, April). Research on applying the concept of electronic performance support system into computer teaching. In *2nd International Conference on Consumer Electronics, Communications and Networks* (pp. 3434–3436). IEEE.
11. Weidong, Z. (2010, September). The application of modern teaching techniques in computer foundation education, In *2010 International Conference on Educational and Information Technology, 2010* (Vol. 1, pp. V1-245–V1-247). IEEE.

Concentrating on Innovation Education to Facilitate Engineering Education

Zufeng Wu, Guobin Zhu, Qihua Wang and Xinyuan Gong

Abstract The chapter introduces the purpose and significance of innovation education and engineering education, and describes the difficulties and confusions encountered in launching engineering education. Finally, it summarizes the positive effects of innovation education in the engineering practice. Innovation education can facilitate engineering education in creating the overall atmosphere, elevating the learning climate, laying the professional basis and improving professional qualities.

Keywords Innovation education · Facilitate · Engineering education

1 Introduction

With the rapid growth of national economy and advance of industry informatization, the lack of innovative talents and advanced engineering personnel becomes a common issue. On one hand, a large number of graduates face their approaching graduations, and on the other hand the search for talented personnel by enterprises cannot be never satisfied because appropriate people are hard to find. In this contradiction, higher education faces significant challenges, i.e., to adapt to the development of society, and cultivate engineering personnel the industry urgently needs, and, finally, be able to carry out innovative work for enterprise. When faced with specific problems, the qualified talents must have ideas, innovations and

Z. Wu · G. Zhu · Q. Wang · X. Gong (✉)
School of Information and Software Engineering, University of Electronic Science and Technology of China, Chengdu, China
e-mail: gongxy@uestc.edu.cn

Z. Wu
e-mail: wuzufeng@uestc.edu.cn

G. Zhu
e-mail: zhugb@uestc.edu.cn

G. Motta and B. Wu (eds.), *Software Engineering Education for a Global E-Service Economy*, Progress in IS, DOI: 10.1007/978-3-319-04217-6_16,
© Springer International Publishing Switzerland 2014

effective implementations. They can find a job as soon as graduation, then go to work, and know how to do as soon as possible.

Innovation is a strategic measure to enhance national competitiveness. More and more countries in the world think innovation as a major strategy [1]. To improve the capability of independent innovation and the level of whole development is our mission that the era endows to us. The goal of the innovation education is to improve the cultivation objects. By cultivating the students' innovative consciousness and thinking, their healthy personality can be developed [2]. In the USA, it's proved effective to let undergraduates participate innovation activities as early as possible through setting seminars and core curriculum to juniors. In China, the innovation education is also taken seriously. In the 2012 National Science and Technology Innovation Conference, as a university president described, the university should seize their own disciplines advantages and characteristics, make the full use of joint point that higher education is the first productive forces of science and technology and personnel as the first resource, and promote the close combination of education, science technology and economy, follow the law of talent development process and scientific research, accelerate the reform pace of the mechanism of scientific and technological system and become the world first-class university eventually in the process of supporting our country independent innovation and service innovation [3]. Li Wei, an outstanding software engineering expert, believes that the cultivation of innovation awareness and capacity of undergraduates should be strengthened [4]. For engineering undergraduate students, how to take advantage of the science and talent resources to cultivate students who can make a huge contribution to the future development to follow the technology trend and industry development is our significant challenge as well as our historical mission. At the same time, we should realize that the traditional type of teaching and the supplement of theoretical knowledge is the basis, but only this cannot inspire more students to grow actively and realize themselves.

In response to the economic globalization, industrial information technology and competitive internationalization trend [5, 6], engineering education, known as a national focus of the education reform measures, gets more and more attention. Engineering education in China started late; the college has laid emphasis on science education. We are lack of understanding of the importance of engineering education to the national development. For example, in enrollment of professional masters, the vast majorities of excellent students compete over the places of academic masters, rather than the professional masters. Some students even give up professional degree master admission and transfer to a lower-scored college in order to gain an academic master degree. Despite constantly strengthened propagation in this aspect, the awareness of the whole society is less than enough. In the European Union, as early as in the 1990s, the completed "European Higher Engineering Education (H3E)", "Enhance the European Engineering Education"(E4), and "Teaching and Research of European Engineering" (TREE) have been known as the trilogy of reshaping engineering education in Europe. These three thematic programs focus on adjusting education structure, studying the practical design content of engineering education teaching activities, enhancing the attractiveness of engineering education, and exploring ways to maintain the survival of engineering education institutions. As early as the establishment of the National Science Foundation (NSF) in 1981, the United States has released national consultation reports to vigorously promote engineering education through National Research Council, National Science Foundation, American Society for Engineering Education, American Academy of Sciences, and American Academy of Engineering. As we all know, with a lot of efforts and explorations, Europe and the United States have made much progress in industrialization and informatization. Germany, France, the United States have been the wonderful examples in the world-wide to be learned from.

2 Explore a New Way of Innovation Education and Engineering Education

Engineering has the following characteristics: sociality, creativity, and comprehensiveness. Engineer's creative and constructive works have the purpose of benefiting mankind, and improving people's life. Therefore it also has moral conditionality and global significance [7, 8]. From the view of the characteristics of engineering, innovation is one of the ways to realize engineering. The software engineering major, as one of the four (branch) subjects of Computing Subject and the supporting subject of software major, will permeate into all computer development projects and play a commanding role [9], In the fall of 1998, the IEEE Computer Society Education Activities Committee and ACM Education Committee released the software engineering subject accreditation report SE2004 [10]. The report scientifically defines the characteristics, knowledge system and curriculum system of the software Engineering Subject. The system refers to the important role of engineering practice in software activities at great length. As a talent-oriented subject, especially in order to meet the challenges of ultra-large-scale software engineering of the network era, emphasis on students' engineering quality and professional practice ability, capabilities of solving problem and managing projects, self-learning ability of adapting to the development of science and technology and subjects' changes and associated comprehensive quality is very important [11]. So innovation education is particularly important for engineering education. Based on a research combining with the actual situation of the students who enrolled in the recent years, we found a certain ratio of students has the following features:

First, lack of learning motivation. Many students turn to become relaxed as soon as they enter the college. They don't find the learning goals, or don't adapt to the state of the self-development from psychological aspect, but still stay in a mind state that just like in high school period, only satisfied by learning theory knowledge, and not caring about other things.

Second, poor in self-learning. Study in the high school is step by step, and students did not form habits of self-management and self-learning. They only cared about quick success and pursued short-term interests. Even if they had a long-term plan, they did not put their plan into real action.

Third, lack of diligence and poor in managing time. In the relatively free environment in university, students spend a lot of time on online games and social contacts. Plus poor self-control and vulnerable to external influence, the time for the students to study is significantly reduced. Besides students do not have a clear plan on time management, or have no actual actions on their plans.

Four, students have high recognition rate on self, occupation and family responsibilities, but are emotional, utilitarian and cannot maintain a long-term good state of mind. They have relatively low responsibility on collectivity and the pragmatism is rather serious. Conflicts between individual interests and collective interests inevitably come out in real engineering practice. Collectivism usually puts the collective interests upon the individual interests; we acknowledge the meaning and value of collectivism. On the other hand, we should also admit the significance and the value of protecting individual, and show some respects for the individual interests and rights, especially the rights of individual life [12].

Both the engineering accreditation by ministry of education and the national excellence engineer program emphasize the coverage of talents cultivation. So, how in this case to complete university education with high-coverage and high-quality, not just only caring about cultivating top students or the talented but ignoring the students who have difficulties, is an urgent problem to solve. Considering the characteristics of engineering education, especially the software engineering, students need to spend a lot of effort and practice in theory study, and hands-on practice. Only in this way they can improve themselves [13]. For example, a large number of software coding error correction and efficiency are achieved by years of experience and accumulation. Only rely on smart cannot solve the problem. That is to say two of the following works should be done perfectly.

To create a good atmosphere for the whole situation, this can influence individuals to learn from model students, and to adapt to the groups.

Construct the platforms and environments and solve the problems of learning approaches by hardware implementation, which can provide a platform and an environment for the students who desire to be the pillar of the society [14].

How to create a good atmosphere? Just simply relying on propaganda and education is not enough; we need real carrier to guide, so we can achieve satisfactory results. Based on the scenario of my school, we are not only active in the students' ideological work, foundation of innovation and entrepreneurship courses, but also carry out following several attempts.

Construct innovation and entrepreneurship center. Build the innovation and entrepreneurship center gradually, establish club by contacting well-known enterprises, and set up interest groups according to the mainstream professional direction. Each club, studio and interest group carry out discussion, project development and funds declaration according to their interest and professional direction, and create a relaxing and free atmosphere in the center. Through years of practice, a number of famous, innovative and entrepreneurial achievements come out. For example, research funding projects, the Youth Innovation Funds of Sichuan Province, good samples of starting a business, and a number of national above contest winners. By propagation of these prototypes, make students participate enthusiastically. Students will consider joining innovation and entrepreneurship center as a symbol of excellent students. Innovation and entrepreneurship center can enroll around 150 people per year.

Set up innovation and entrepreneurship funds. Establish innovation and entrepreneurship funds to encourage students to realize their thoughts, so as to inspire them to participate voluntarily and actively, instead of passive management. Adopting the whole process of scientific research project management, i.e., filling in project declaration, and then defense, expert approval, project publicity, mission statement signature, mid-term defense, and concluding defense, students could benefit a lot from industry investigation, project declaration, process management, communication, and feasibility study. Through this process, students can transit from passive experimental experience to team management. This fund's intention not only lies in enhancing students' skills, but more importantly is to make students think actively, and improve innovation awareness, as well as the capacity of project development [15, 16]. Judging from the record of the past, we have about 40 projects a year, an average of five students responsible for each project; in total we can have coverage about 200 students.

Establish enterprise virtual class. We build up the new mechanism of letting companies be closely involved in the personnel training. Through the process of companies' lecture, mentor guidance, knowledge supplement, campus training, internship training and a series of cultivation process in accordance with the actual level of the students, we have enhanced students' understanding of the industry, enterprise, their professions, and improved the ability of project engineering. We also have made students clear about their future career planning, completed seamless connect with enterprise in advance. In the real practice, we find that many students still have the idea to learn, but they hardly have the chance to contact with enterprises, and form the real understanding of the way in actual engineering practice. But through this platform, nearly 200 students get involved, and the result is pretty promising.

Head-teacher responsibility mechanism. Set up the system that every teacher has the responsibility to cultivate students; each administrative class has a head-teacher, who has the natural advantages in professional quality and life experience. The teacher has the chance to initiate professional guidance, ideological education, guide students, and help difficult students hand in hand, take a close look at students' difficulties, and carry out learning and life guidance in accordance with the situation [17]. Especially in the area where the ideological instructor can't reach, they play a considerable role in professional studies, research abilities and professional qualities.

A lot of real practice has proved that there is no one kind of measure that could take all into consideration. Situation of each student varies, so a variety of measures and work from different angles are necessary [18, 19].

3 Build the High Level Education Platform with the Help of Well-Known Companies

Although a variety of measures has been taken and solved the connection problem between schools and enterprises to some extent, how to make the students be able to contact the leading international companies in the industry, broaden their horizons, grasp the mainstream of corporation environment and technology, and enhance international competitiveness, we need to think about the problem seriously [20]. Through the internship project we let students experience the international development environment and procedures, gain real practice experience, and build foundation for the following internship,

Declaring together with IBM, the IBM technology center of our school has obtained the title as the state-level engineering practice education center. We also have introduced IBM UTP program, classes taught by senior IBM engineer, and have built the IBM virtual development environment.

We have built the joint laboratory with the world's largest enterprise management software provider SAP. Establish the student practical enterprise ERP sandbox in our school. Through the SAP experiment environment, our students will become familiar with enterprise management software development and process, and enjoy the opportunity of ecological circle project practice and training opportunities with payment from SAP [21]. Through the SAP PA certification exam, students can join SAP reserve pool and share the global scope of employment opportunity.

We have also built the joint laboratory with the world's largest database software provider Oracle. Through the construction of development of environment from software to hardware, and the establishment of student cultivation demonstration center, we have promoted students' engineering skills, systematic thinking and analytical capabilities.

4 Conclusions

Software engineering, as a highly engineered discipline, is always the focus of engineering education. Through a lot of innovation education and work measures, we have seen the gradual formation participation atmosphere of everyone in our school. And these ways are commenced by surrounding the goal of professional learning, and practice in software engineering. Through different types of platform training, team training, presentation training, and professional competence training, we have brought our students to join in the project voluntarily, so that students could benefit a lot from the atmosphere which emphasizes the engineering training and study. As for the future, students could lay a solid foundation when doing internship, curriculum design and project training plan.

To sum up, as long as we start the strategy based on disciplines features, we could let innovation education play a vital role in building up the whole atmosphere, enhancing the learning atmosphere, laying the basis of professional studies, and improving professional qualities. Finally, innovation education acts as an assistant role in carrying out and promoting engineering education smoothly.

References

1. Xu, H. (2009). The standard evaluation in high school innovative people cultivation. *Jiangsu higher education*, (6), 107–108.
2. Zhu, H. (2011). The famous American undergraduates innovation education evaluation. *Chinese university teaching*, (10), 90–95.
3. Wan, Y. (2012). Higher education institutions should contribute to establishing innovation-oriented country. *China Education Daily*, 2012-7-9(1).
4. Li, W. (2006). Deepen the educational reform to promote high-quality innovative personnel training. *Beijing Education*, (4), 23–25.
5. Lyons, W. C. (2000). U.S. and international engineering education: A vision of engineering's future. *Journal of Professional Issues in Engineering Education and Practice*, (10), 152–155.
6. Grandin, J. M. (2006). Preparing engineers for the global workplace [EB/OL]. *Online Journal for Global Engineering Education*, 1(1). http://digitalcommons.uri.edu/ojgee/vol1/iss1/3
7. Xiang, H. (2007). About reforming engineering education and cultivate innovative people. *Research in Higher Education of Engineering*, (5), 1–23. http://wanfang.uestc.edu.cn/C/periodical-zgaqkxxb.aspx
8. ACM/IEEE. (2001). The Joint Task Force. Computing Currieula 2001—Computer Science [EB/OL]. http://www.computer.org/edueation/cc2001/final/, November 15, 2001.
9. Gao, L. (2010). Software elites is so tempered. *Higher Education Press*, 179–180.
10. ACM/IEEE. (2004). The joint task force. Software Engineering 2004. http://sites.Eomputer.org/ccse/%5BEB/OL%5D, August 23, 2004.
11. Zhichang, Q., & Qingping, T. (2012). Software engineering education: Facing the challenge of ultra-system in net era. *China University Teaching*, (3), 23–25.
12. Fan, J. (2011). Engineer's social responsibility in engineering education: Content, evolution and cultivation. *Modern Education Administration*, (1), 75–78.
13. Software Engineering 2004. Curriculum guidelines for undergraduate degree programs in software engineering [EB/OL]. http://sites.computer.org/ccse/
14. Ultra-Large-Scale Systems: The software challenge of the future (ISBN 0-9786956-0-7) [EB/OL]. http://www.smartulss.com/.
15. Defang, L. (2009). Penetrating innovation education into the whole process of engineering talents cultivation. *China University Education*, (12), 50–52.
16. Gaofeng, Z. (2007). Innovation and engineering education. *Higher Engineering Education Research*, (1).
17. Gaofeng, Z. (2007). Innovative talents and engineering education reform, (6).
18. Shen, X. (2008). Attention to improve practical skills and engineering education level. *Chinese Higher Education*, (2).
19. Gaofeng, Z. (2011). Present state and perspective of Chinese Engineering Education, (6).

20. Xiuying, Z., Jiang, G., & Fu, Z. (2008). Implementing specialty accreditation, promoting quality of engineering education. *China University Education*, (12).
21. Jin, F., Yan, D., & Zhenyan, L. (2011). Exploration on modes of engineering practical ability of software engineering undergraduates. *Computer Engineering and Science*, (S1), 139–141.

Student-Centered Course Development of Digital Media Technology

Tonghua Su, Peijun Ma, Shengchun Deng, Dong Li and Hujie Huang

Abstract We illustrate the student-centered teaching paradigm using a case study on the course development of digital media technology. The success key is fourfold. First, the teaching subjects and course objective should be determined. In light of this consideration, we can cipher out who are the users of our teaching. Second, a deliberated class design should be undertaken. Third, the practice activity system should be established. Finally, the evaluation metrics should be defined which are valuable to improve the future classes. The effectiveness of the paradigm is verified through evaluations.

Keywords Course development · Student-centered teaching · Software engineering education · User needs · Digital media technology

1 Introduction

Digital Media Technology is an introductory course for School of Software at Harbin Institute of Technology. Digital media technologies are changing the way we conduct our private, social and business lives, and transforming our experience

T. Su (✉) · P. Ma · S. Deng · D. Li · H. Huang
School of Software, Harbin Institute of Technology, Harbin, China
e-mail: thsu@hit.edu.cn

P. Ma
e-mail: ma@hit.edu.cn

S. Deng
e-mail: dsc@hit.edu.cn

D. Li
e-mail: Lee@hit.edu.cn

H. Huang
e-mail: hjhuang@hit.edu.cn

G. Motta and B. Wu (eds.), *Software Engineering Education for a Global E-Service Economy*, Progress in IS, DOI: 10.1007/978-3-319-04217-6_17, © Springer International Publishing Switzerland 2014

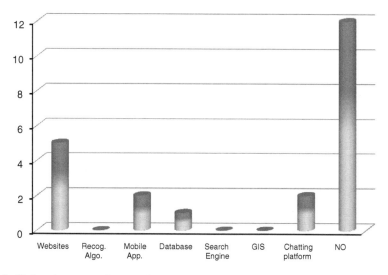

Fig. 1 Students' programming experiences

of media out of all recognition. This course covers a spectrum of topics from core techniques supporting digital media, investigating how this has come about. By the end of the studies, students will understand the direction how to keep on top of future developments.

The development process of the course includes four steps. Foremost, determine the needs of students who are our teaching subjects. Then a tailored syllabus can be designed. The third step is to design a deliberated practice assurance system. The final effectiveness can be achieved unless multidimensional teaching tools and effective designs are associated. As the last step, the evaluation metrics should be defined. These metrics are critical to evaluate whether the teaching fulfill its objective.

The next section discusses the students' needs. In Sects. 3 and 4, the class design and practice activity design are detailed. Section 5 provides resultant evaluations. Finally, brief conclusions are given.

2 User Requirement Analysis

Requirement analysis is the critical step in software development. It showed that 45 % of the failures are due to defective requirement [1]. The requirements of students play the same role in teaching design.

We first determined the "users" of our teaching. They are twenty graduate students majoring in digital media and information retrieval. Their experiences can be divided as websites design, recognition algorithm design, mobile application development, database development, search engine practice, GIS programming, chatting platform development. In our poll, only a few of them have experiences as in Fig. 1.

3 Class Design

A tailored class design plays an important role for a successful course development. Our design includes teaching attitude, syllabus, and teaching contents. All the while, we adopt a student centred principle.

As for teaching attitude, teachers should believe that students want to learn, and they assume, until proven otherwise, that they can. Ken Bain has said that best teaching can be found not in particular practices or rules but in the attitudes of the teachers, in their faith in their students' abilities to achieve, in their willingness to take their students seriously and to let them assume control of their own education [2].

The course aims to reveal the recent development in the digital media fields covering the media representation, data compression, massive data management, intelligent software development, mobile media development and intelligent web design. We have collected students' interests in these topics (see Fig. 2). According to the students' preferences in Fig. 2, we changed the sessions of each topic. The main points of our syllabus are listed as follows:

Lecture 1 Introduction to digital media technologies (2 sessions): Concept of digital media, scope of the course, key technologies for digital media; innovative applications of digital media technologies.

Lecture 2 Hardware and operating systems (2 sessions): Capture devices, input/output devices for digital media, and a variety of sensors for Internet of Things, Microsoft Kinect; Desktop OS, Smartphone OS and node OS, Windows and Unix, Android and iOS, TinyOS and MOS.

Lecture 3 Theories and techniques for media representation (3 sessions): Sampling theory and information theory, how to sample and quantize continuous signals, how to reconstruct continuous signals; Measurement of information, capacity of information, Shannon's theorem, representation techniques for audio, image, and video.

Lecture 4 Data compression technology (3 sessions): The generic techniques for data compression, Uniform quantization, optimum quantization, Huffman coding, run-length coding, arithmetic coding, dictionary-based coding, predictive coding; the compression standard for audio, image and video.

Lecture 5 Massive data management technology (4 sessions): The new challenges in "big data" and "digital universe", three kinds of traditional data storage structures, why data center is in urgent demand? Review the international standard for data center, Google file system, MapReduce and BigTable, Hadoop, large-scale word counting.

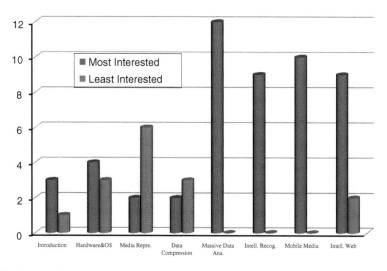

Fig. 2 Students' interests

Lecture 6 Intelligent learning and prediction technology (6 sessions): Concepts of Pattern Recognition, components of a Pattern Recognition system, feature extraction and model learning, learning vector quantization and its application to handwriting recognition, the application of intelligent recognition theory in biometric tasks and Microsoft Kinect motion-sensing system.

Lecture 7 Mobile media technology (4 sessions): The trends of the smartphone and OS, core technologies of mobile communications; case study of novel mobile apps: mobile navigator, 2D barcode reader; mobile programming.

Lecture 8 Intelligent web technology (4 sessions): The scenarios of intelligent web and its concept, the components of intelligent web; Searching engine and ranking algorithms; typical recommendation system: its principles, its algorithms, its procedures for successful deployments.

4 Practice Activity Design

We have carefully designed the practice activities. The student centred learning associates closely with teamwork, interactive communication and discussion. In the first class, students are required to create their groups around 2–4 persons. Slides, homework, and projects are prepared to reach the course objective. For example, there are 10 novel projects for their choice. Each group can select the most interested one as their test bed and struggle to be experts in that topic.

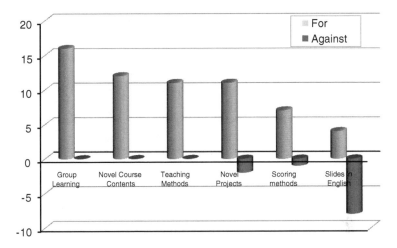

Fig. 3 Evaluation of students': **a** benefits and **b** opinion

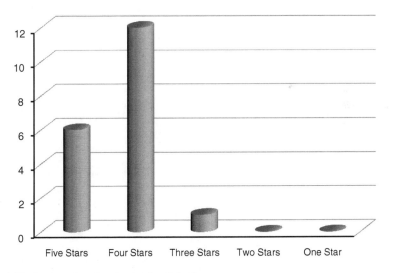

Fig. 4 Evaluation of students' overall satisfaction

We take the homework assignment as an example to illustrate special strategies used by this course. The score on one assignment is shared by the whole group, that is, each group just submits one copy of answer produced collectively. During the scoring process, it is done in class by another group. In this way, they have the chance to understand the assignments in depth.

5 Evaluation

We investigate the following two questions: (1) What benefits did you obtained from the course? (2) Which features should be kept/discarded? The results are outlined in Fig. 3. We can see that most students have benefits in theory foundation, practice training and teamwork. Similarly, all students support the groupwise learning methods, novel course contents, and teaching methods. Few students complain about the high difficulties of projects. Some of the students cannot follow the slides in English smoothly. We will add more comments in Chinese to reduce the difficulties of reading slides in the next time. We have also collected the students' satisfaction. It is over 94 % as showed in Fig. 4. It validates the success of this course.

6 Conclusions

This chapter presents the four-step course development paradigm. Its process is illustrated during the case study on digital media technology. All the while, students are always centred to design the class and syllabus. The evaluation verified the effectiveness of the paradigm.

References

1. Schach, S. R. (2010). *Object-oriented and classical software engineering*. New York: McGraw-Hill.
2. Bain, K. (2004). *What the best college teachers do*. Cambridge: Harvard University Press.

International Master on Manufacturing Service Ecosystem: A Proposal

David Chen and Jean-Paul Bourrieres

Abstract This chapter tentatively proposes to establish an international master programme on Manufacturing Service Ecosystem. The content of the proposed master curriculum is based on an on-going European FP7 Integrated Project MSEE (Manufacturing Service EcosystEm). The MSEE project will be first outlined in the paper. The curriculum of the proposed master programme will then be presented and discussed in detail. Perspective will be given as part of the conclusion.

Keywords Enterprise modeling · Service · Service engineering · International master

1 Introduction

Most of existing master programmes in France and in European countries do not have an explicit service engineering orientation in the context of manufacturing domain. To keep competiveness of European industry in the world global market, there is a need to shift from traditional manufacturing engineering based training curriculum to manufacturing service orientation in a virtual enterprise environment and ecosystem. This chapter tentatively exploits the opportunity to create in University Bordeaux 1 an international master on manufacturing service ecosystem in order to provide to the market place a new type of engineers dedicated to manufacturing related service system engineering in networked environment. The proposal is based on the concepts and some outcomes of MSEE project [1].

D. Chen (✉) · J.-P. Bourrieres
Laboratoire de l'Intégration du Matériau au Système, University of Bordeaux,
Talence, France
e-mail: david.chen@ims-bordeaux.fr

J.-P. Bourrieres
e-mail: Jean-Paul.Bourrieres@ims-bordeaux.fr

G. Motta and B. Wu (eds.), *Software Engineering Education for a Global E-Service Economy*, Progress in IS, DOI: 10.1007/978-3-319-04217-6_18,
© Springer International Publishing Switzerland 2014

MSEE is an Integrated Project of the ICT Work Programme under the European Community's 7th Framework Programme (FP7). The project aims to create a new Virtual Factory Industrial Models, where service orientation and collaborative innovation will support a new renaissance of Europe in the global manufacturing context. The vision hold by MSEE is by 2015, novel service-oriented management methodologies and the Future Internet universal business infrastructure will enable European virtual factories and enterprises to self-organize in distributed, autonomous, interoperable, non-hierarchical innovation ecosystems of tangible and intangible manufacturing assets, to be virtually described, on-the-fly composed and dynamically delivered as a Service, end-to-end along the globalised value chain [2]. This vision stems upon two complementary pillars, which have characterized the last 10 years of research about Virtual Organizations, Factories and Enterprises: Service Oriented Architectures (SOA) and Digital Business Ecosystems (DBE).

2 Basic Concepts

The proposed master aims at supporting the servitization process from traditional manufacturing enterprise to service in virtual enterprise and ecosystem. This servitization concept is also the baseline of MSEE project and is better described by Thoben [3]. Figure 1 illustrates this servitization process from tangible product to intangible services around product and finally service as product. It characteristics our view clearly focuses on extending a formerly tangible product to intangible ones.

3 Objective

The objective of the proposed international master is twofold. First it aims at educating a new generation of young engineers on manufacturing servitization related concepts, models, methodologies and tools. Second the proposed curriculum also applies for vocational training purpose to transform traditional manufacturing system engineers to manufacturing service ecosystem experts. Both aim at helping European industry to develop intangible products in order to better gain competitiveness of tangible ones in the market.

More concretely, the proposed master will train high level executives in «Service System Architects» in VME and Ecosystem context, capable of: innovating, modelling, designing, implementing organizational/technical solution to support the entire servitization process to improve the competiveness of manufacturing companies; and evolving/working in an international professional environment.

The employments mainly concern the companies (large companies as well as SMEs) implemented in international market that desire to develop services around

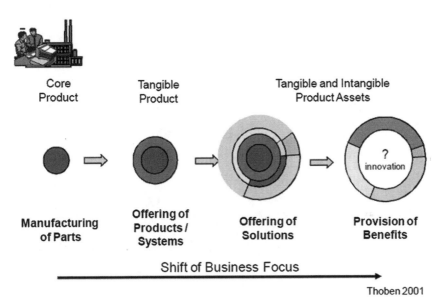

Fig. 1 MSE service-product concept

their manufactured products. The positions are situated in the sector of manu-facturing industry as well as that of the services: Responsible person in charge of servitization, service lifecycle management (innovation, design, implementation, delivery, maintenance), person in charge of product and service integration, servitization consultant, servization project leader etc.

4 Overview of the Master Programme

The proposed master programme is built on 1 year training curriculum (Year 5). It consists in two semesters (corresponding to semesters 9 and 10 of university lifecycle). The semester 9 is lectures and exercises in classroom and semester 10 consists in project and internship. Figure 2 gives an overview on the modules and ECTS (European Credit Transfer System) of each module.

- Service and servitization (S&S): This module provides basic concepts and definitions on service (particularly manufacturing service) and servitization. The models and methods related to service in virtual enterprise and ecosystem are studied as well as the servitization process. (Service science, servitization framework, Ecosystem, VME (Virtual Manufacturing enterprise).
- Service system modeling (SSM): It aims at presenting main enterprise modeling (EM) techniques and service modeling languages. Those EM include decision system model (GRAI), function and process description formalisms in IDEF0

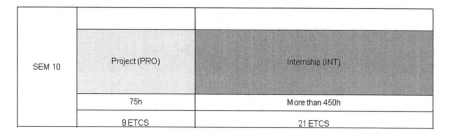

SEM 9	Service and servitization (S&S)	Service system modeling (SSM)	Service system design (SSD)	Service performance evaluation (SPE)	Service lifecycle management (SLM)	Service innovation (SIN)
	25h	50h	50h	25h	50h	50h
	3 ECTS	6 ECTS	6 ECTS	3 ECTS	6 ECTS	6 ECTS

SEM 10	Project (PRO)	Internship (INT)
	75h	More than 450h
	9 ETCS	21 ETCS

Fig. 2 Overview of the master on manufacturing service ecosystem

and IDEF3, MDSEA (Model Driven Service Engineering Architecture) and associated service system modeling languages developed in MSEE project, as well as USDL (Unified Service Description Language) etc.

- Service system design (SSD): This module consists in service engineering framework and methodology, service design principles and rules, service system simulation methods and tools, ServLab and other service testing methods.
- Service performance evaluation (SPE): It gives concepts on service quality and performance evaluation. Methods to implement performance indicators (PI) and SLAs such as ECOGRAI method and VRM will be studied. Case studies will be carried out to learn how to choose KPIs.
- Service lifecycle management (SLM): SLM will be studied and compared with PLM (Product Lifecycle Management) to show similarity and possible activities to be coordinated and synchronized between the two lifecycles. Available relevant service models, methods and tools will be synthesized along SLM phases with the help of SLM framework to show the role they play and stakeholders involved. Tangible and intangible assets virtualization methods will also be included.
- Service innovation (SIN): This module gives basic concepts and principles on service innovation in VME and Ecosystem environments. Existing service innovation framework, models and methods will be presented and studied in detail. Focus of the study will be given on product oriented service innovation in manufacturing context as well as synergy and relationship to traditional manufacturing product innovation.

5 Conclusions

This chapter has tentatively proposed to develop an international master on manufacturing service in Virtual Enterprise and Ecosystem. Service oriented education is relatively new in traditional higher education establishments. The international orientation of the proposed master has two aspects; first it aims at educating future young engineers capable of evolving in a international working environment, second the master programme requires international collaboration in order to support international internships and provide with the best available knowledge and international teaching staffs.

This international master can be also considered as an accompanying action with respect to MSEE project. It allows going beyond the project duration to sustain and exploit MSEE project results after the MSEE project completion.

Acknowledgments Authors of the paper thank and acknowledge all partners of MSEE project consortium for their contribution to the project.

References

1. Manufacturing SErvice ecosystem (MSEE). (2011). Annex I—Description of work. MSEE consortium, 2011-04-29.
2. European Commission, MSEE project overview, http://www.msee-ip.eu/project-overview/msee-vision
3. Thoben, K.-D., Jagdev, H., & Eschenbächer, J. (2001). Extended products: Evolving traditional product concepts. In: K.-D. Thoben, F. Weber & K. S. Pawar (Eds.), *Proceedings of the 7th International Conference on Concurrent Enterprising: "Engineering the Knowledge Economy through Co-operation"* Bremen, Germany, June 2001.

Service Science and Scholarship: Experiences from a Pragmatist Perspective

Gianluigi Viscusi, Marco Cremaschi and Carlo Batini

Abstract This chapter discusses the case of ongoing experiences in the field of Service Science. The experiences refer to the Italian SMART project producing a homonymous methodology, briefly described together with a discussion of its application as an instrument for developing and structuring initiatives in Service Science education and in the design of services in funded industrial research projects. The discussion follows a pragmatist perspective, focusing on the enactment of a "funded experience" by scholars, practitioners, and Service Science students.

Keywords Service science · Pragmatism · Scholarship · Methodology

1 Introduction

In the last 5 years, Service Science [1] has evolved from a pioneering field to an emerging multidisciplinary research area, attaining a growing mainstream resonance and scientific recognition [2, 3]. Notwithstanding the progress, several issues are still open as for Service Science Education and Scholarship: in particular, the challenges still concern the development and recognition of (1) a common understanding of Service Science core skills, (2) career path, (3) the relevance of both pure and applied research [3].

G. Viscusi · M. Cremaschi · C. Batini (✉)
Department of Informatics, Systems and Communication (Disco),
University of Milano-Bicocca, Milan, Italy
e-mail: batini@disco.unimib.it

G. Viscusi
e-mail: viscusi@disco.unimib.it

M. Cremaschi
e-mail: marco.cremaschi@disco.unimib.it

G. Motta and B. Wu (eds.), *Software Engineering Education for a Global E-Service Economy*, Progress in IS, DOI: 10.1007/978-3-319-04217-6_19,
© Springer International Publishing Switzerland 2014

As for this last point, it is our believe that a pragmatist perspective [4], grounding and selecting theory on the basis of social conventions and their usefulness in the current service ecosystem, may provide a suitable alternative for both academic and practitioners. Indeed, a focus on what Dewey called "funded experience" [5], would be the appropriate underlying philosophy for an effective learning of what is and how to put in practice what is at the core of the Service Science, namely the service-dominant logic, S-D logic [6, 7]. To this end in the following we discuss the experience carried out in the SMART project (Services and Meta-services for SMART eGovernment) for the design, the application, and the teaching of a methodological framework. We point out the interest of the case because of the duality of the relationships between the different activities; on the one hand, the design influences the structuring of the learning modules and goals; on the other hand, learning and business applications of the framework contribute to enrich the very same structure and features of the methodology itself.

Thus, in the following we first briefly introduce state of the art methodologies and approaches to service design and planning, together with the current issues of Service Science scholarship and learning. Then, we provide an overview of the SMART methodology, subsequently described in its application in higher education courses and in design of value added services for agro food sector in Italy. Finally, a summary of the discussed experience concludes the chapter.

2 Background and Motivations

Service Science education faces the challenge of the development of both new skills and configuration of available skills in several areas, such as business models and processes, science and technology, people and culture, thus combining people, technology, value and clients [8]. The consolidation of the area is currently an ongoing challenge reflected by the number of frameworks and modelling efforts available in the contributing disciplines, such as information systems (IS), service marketing, service engineering and computing. Considering the IS literature, [9] discusses a four layer service domain framework to support the understanding, analysing, and researching service topics across different research areas. Furthermore, [10, 11] propose respectively a meta-model approach to service systems and an integrated view of service marketing, service operations, and service computing, arguing that Service Science should not privilege "servitizing" over "productizing", and that the concept of customer should be not simplified but better considered as made up of different groups and types of customers. Finally, [12] presents a framework for design research in the Service Science discipline, allowing for the systematisation of research regarding the design and evaluation of innovative IT artefacts in the Service Science discipline.

Other contributions from computer science focus on studying the very nature of service, on the one hand, to provide a general service model to unambiguously describe services towards a shared conceptualization [13]; on the other hand, to make available a foundation for designing, producing, delivering, operating, maintaining, monitoring, and improving service systems under a market-oriented and economic growth perspective [14].

Notwithstanding these multidisciplinary efforts the design and planning of services in digital service ecosystems still sees a focus on the technological perspective as the prevailing one. Indeed, the Service Oriented Computing (SOC) paradigm and service oriented design and development methodologies support the realization of service-based ICT infrastructures [15–17], covering only one perspective among the many considered in initiatives aimed at designing and planning services in service ecosystems. As pointed out by [18], a service ecosystem is a marketplace for trading services in which services are developed, published, sold and used; accordingly, design and evaluation frameworks are required, considering all the different features of a service ecosystem: from technology to social and psychological issues implied by the service experience. As for these issues, an integration of the marketing focus in new engineering and technology oriented perspectives on services is necessary in order to provide service designers with insights into consumers' perception of service convenience and services consumption experience, see for example [19, 20].

Moving to service engineering, the need for software engineers to first understand a service, its ecosystem, and business models to build effective systems supporting it, contributes to promote a growing focus on strategy engineering and modelling the enterprise's goals and intentions that motivate the exchange of economically valuable things [21]. As a consequence, new models and frameworks have been proposed in literature based on the awareness of the difference between service systems and traditional software engineering (SE) approaches [22] and the need for a proper alignment between business and IT, a service perspective at the business level [23].

The above discussion provides a general idea of the challenge of having first a comprehensive understanding of all issues and factors impacting or else having an influence on the design, planning, and development of services supported and or delivered by information and communication technologies through environment, heavily characterised by digital constituents. Furthermore, education in Service Science faces the same challenges, requiring frameworks and instruments characterised by a certain kind of homology with the design, planning, and development activities. The first motivation is the continuity between education and professional skills and capabilities: briefly we argue here for an approach and perspective close on the one hand to methods as the Engaged Scholarship discovery, teaching, application, and integration [24–26]; on the other to design approaches inspired by action research [27].

A major challenge concerns again the consideration of service ecosystems under a holistic perspective, whereas silos oriented perspectives on the different subsystems prevail, still grounded in the above mentioned disciplinary boundaries [28]. Furthermore, moving between subsystems asks for filling conceptual and ontological gaps, e.g., between the technological system of Web services (WSs) and the organizational system [28]. Nevertheless, as for these issues, at the state of the art different proposals have been discussed, focusing, for example, on the use of conceptual models to map and manage the complexity of service systems, both for learning [29] and design activities [28], where the aim is to map high-level goals to tasks addressed in technology oriented perspectives such as, e.g., the above mentioned service oriented computing.

In the following we discuss the case of the SMART methodology, aiming to connect scholarship in Service Science and professional activities by means of its exploitation in essays production, learning case studies, and service design activities in funded industrial projects. Thus, first we briefly introduce the conceptual model and the different phases of the SMART methodology; then we outline some of the applications of the methodology to scholarship and learning initiatives.

3 The SMART Methodology

The SMART methodology is the result of research efforts carried out in a homonymous Italian project of industrial research and development (Services and Meta-Services for smART eGovernment—SMART). The project aims at produce digital services for both private and public sector, developing at the same time a formalisation of the activities in term of a methodology. This latter is intended to define a procedural path for the life cycle of planning, design, production, sale, use, management and monitoring of services, from the point of view of three main actors: the *planner* (e.g., a Public Administration), the *service provider* (e.g., again a Public Administration or else a private broker), and the *user of the service*.

The focus of the methodology is the concept of value, in its various meanings, among others: public value (e.g., for a Public Administration), exchange value (for the provider) and value in use (for the end-user). The methodology is the evolution of the eG4M methodology, formerly designed for strategic planning of e-Government services [30–32], thus extending it to a broader domain of application and target adopters.

The methodology is further based on a conceptual model called iPAS, which extends the one proposed in [33, 34], mainly focused on government to business services. The resulting SMART methodology consists of five phases:

1. *Planning* in which the individual planner defines the strategic long-term activities in the production and delivery of services.
2. *Reconstruction* of the different components of the service system and of the relationships among them, with an evaluation of the level of service quality and value in use for the users.
3. *Design* in which the architectural choices and processes are taken.
4. *Production* in which the services are specified and service processes are realized.

Table 1 Steps of the planning phase

Steps	Description
1.1 Strategic planning	The step identifies and defines the principles and policies of the service initiative
1.2 Requirements analysis	The step identifies and models the goals of the end users

5. *Exercise* in which services are delivered, and the resources for the maintenance or renovation of service levels are provided; in this phase a monitoring of the quality and usefulness of services to end users is carried out.

The five phases are made up of different steps; in the Table 1 we provide as an example a high-level description of the steps that make up the *Planning* phase.

The step of strategic planning (1.1) defines the main priorities identified by the provider, for example, to promote the services within e-mail and backup through a cloud solution (technological goal), or to direct the production and supply of services to disabled users (social goal). The step of requirements analysis (1.2) then produces a set of goals or objectives of the users, and a first set of services that allow achieving these goals.

As a further example of the different perspectives considered in the SMART methodology, we now provide a brief discussion of the phase of *Reconstruction of the system of services*, which aims at providing an integrated view of all levels of the ecosystem services. Here the steps considered are eReadiness analysis, quality assessment, and value assessment of services.

eReadiness is usually measured in e-Government planning [35] to identify the initiatives to be taken to promote the adoption of the digital innovation by the different sectors of society involved in the delivery of services; the step also produces a user segmentation in homogeneous categories. The quality assessment of quality identifies the most important dimensions to consider in the service initiative, and then measure them by using objective and subjective metrics, possibly by comparing the values with national or international benchmarking. Finally, the step of assessment of the value of the services measures the value in use as perceived by the end users.

In the following section we first provide an account of the application of the methodology as both learning and working tool. Subsequently, we discuss a case study of its use in service design activities in funded industrial projects.

4 Applications

The SMART methodology is currently adopted under an action research approach in the design of e-Government services, involving academics, practitioners from both public and private companies, and public managers.

Table 2 Phases and related core disciplines

Phases	Core disciplines
Planning	• Management of information systems
	• Requirements engineering
	• Strategy and innovation management
	• Policy making and decision sciences
	• Service science (introduction)
Reconstruction of the system of services	• Business modelling
	• Quality management
	• Service management
	• Social studies of information systems
Design	• Human computer interaction
	• Information management
	• Systems analysis and design
Production	• Business process management
	• Data engineering
	• Service engineering
	• Software engineering
Exercise	• Business intelligence
	• Marketing
	• Operations research

The results of the design activities in terms of requirements, case studies, as well as the above mentioned stakeholders are used in a parallel set of education activities, consisting in:

• a Master on ICT management provided to students in a blended e-learning way (Length: 6 months).
• a Postgraduate Professional Course on Service Science (Length: 1 year).

The two initiatives have involved since March 2012 nearly 50 students, and have been structured following the phases of the methodology and the corresponding disciplines as shown in Table 2.

As also mentioned above, it is worth noting that the two courses involved managers from the organisations participating to the SMART project, discussing with students and scholars the issues at stake in the concurrent service design activities. Some of these issues have been the focus of class exercises and lectures, as well of the final examination essay, consisting in the instantiation of the methodology on a proposal for local and central administrations e-Government services.

The choice of this type of examination is inherited from previous experiences of application of the original eG4M methodology, whose SMART is an evolution and extension. As in the case of eG4M students, the resulting plans required an average of two man-weeks [36].

5 Case Study

This section will describe how the methodology has been adopted in the Mobile Services for Agrofood (MoSeForAgrofood) research project, leading to the design and implementation of "Smart Label" service. The project, partially funded by the Lombardy Region (Italy), involved four Italian Universities: University of Milano-Bicocca, University of Milano, Politecnico di Milano, University of Insubria. Moreover, MoSeForAgrofood aimed to address quality issues in planning, design and provision of value added mobile services. Thus, the project deployed a set of prototype services, among which we consider the "Smart Label" one, delivered through a *mobile app*, providing consumers more information than traditional food label. Accordingly, the app is suitable to support healthier and informed food choices. In the following we discuss how the SMART methodology has been applied for the elicitation of the requirements, the design, and the subsequent deployment of the SMART label.

Considering, the *Planning phase* of the SMART methodology, the focus on requirements engineering methods for goal and intentions modelling [37, 38] allows the elicitation of general properties and qualities characterizing consumers' buying behaviour. However, in the *Reconstruction of the system of service*, through an analysis of the agrofood economic literature, we have further identified some consumer clusters, characterized by similar needs. These led to the organization of focus groups in order to assess the perceived value [39] of "Smart Label" service, whose results provide evidence of consumers' interest in having more information about the products they buy and how this need is satisfied just in a small part by traditional labels. Furthermore, the analysis of the outputs of these early phases of the SMART methodology also manifests how the current food labels are actually characterized by a low level of clarity and transparency. The information gathered from the focus groups together with additional field work by supermarkets in Lombardy were used to identify the types of information considered interesting and relevant to the consumer. Finally, the identification of types of information allows having a support for the maximization of the value of the "Smart Label" service.

In conclusion, this application of the SMART methodology allows evidencing critical issues for service request and fruition, showing that users require further technologies that anticipate their needs, simplify the service interaction, improve accessibility of the effective use of information. Taking these issues into account, and considering the wide spread of mobile telephony (which offers an opportunity to develop electronic value-added-services [40]) in the *Design* phase the "Smart Label" service has been conceived for being provided through an app characterized by Near Field Communication technology (NFC) [41]. The main value of NFC is related to its capacity to enable mediation and activation of many services in a particularly user-friendly way, enhancing the accessibility of services for different types of potential users. As for the value optimization, simulations of "Smart Label" adoption and use actually point out that this service may offer substantial benefits to consumers and businesses in the agrofood cluster; in particular, the chance for consumers to access additional contents (e.g., recipes, personalized information, etc.), and the capability for businesses to guarantee the accountability of both their production processes and the genuineness of products.

6 Conclusion

This chapter aims to discuss an ongoing experience in the field of Service Science. The experience refers to the Italian SMART project, producing a homonymous methodology, briefly described in the previous sections together with a discussion of its application as an instrument for developing and structuring initiatives in Service Science education.

It is our point that this kind of use of the methodology represents a way to enhance scholarship as "funded experience", because of the duality of the relationships of the different activities; on the one hand, the design influences the structuring of the learning modules and goals; on the other hand, learning and business applications of the framework as in the case of the MoSeForAgrofood project contribute to a more appropriate design of services, fitting with contextual requirements and needs, enriching at the same time both the structure and features of the methodology itself.

Acknowledgments The work presented in this chapter has been partially supported by the Italian PON project PON01_00861 SMART (Services and Meta-services for SMART eGovernment) and by Lombardy Region framework agreement 14629/RCC Mobile Services for Agro-Food (MoSeForAgrofood).

References

1. Chesbrough, H., & Spohrer, J. (2006). A research manifesto for services science. *Communications of the ACM, 49*(7), 35–40.
2. Lusch, R., & Wu, C. (2012). A service science perspective on higher education—Linking service productivity theory and higher education reform.
3. Ovum, IBM, & Aalto University'. (2010). Making service science mainstream—A white paper based on the 2009 service science summit.
4. Rorty, R. (1982). *Consequences of pragmatism: Essays, 1972–1980* (p. 237). University of Minnesota Press.
5. Dewey, J. (1938). *Experience and education* (pp. xii, 2 l., 116 p.). Simon and Schuster.
6. Vargo, S. L., & Akaka, M. A. (2009). Service-dominant logic as a foundation for service science: Clarifications. *Science, 1*(1), 32–41.
7. Vargo, S. L., & Lusch, R. F. (2008). Service-dominant logic: Continuing the evolution. *Journal of the Academy of Marketing Science, 36*(1), 1–10.
8. Murphy, W., & Hefley, B. (2008). Service science, management and engineering education. In *World Computer Congress Industry Conference*.
9. Alter, S. (2009). Mapping the domain of service science. *Information Systems Journal*, 1–16.

10. Alter, S. (2011). Metamodel for service design and service innovation: Integrating service activities, service systems, and value constellations. In *ICIS 2011 Proceedings*.
11. Alter, S. (2012). Challenges for service science. *Journal of Information Technology Theory and Application, 13*(2), 22–37.
12. Becker, J., Beverungen, D., Knackstedt, R., Matzner, M., Mueller, O., & Poeppelbuss, J. (2009). A framework for design research in the service science discipline. In *AMCIS 2009 Proceedings*.
13. Ferrario, R., Guarino, N., Janiesch, C., Kiemes, T., Oberle, D., & Probst, F. (2011). Towards an ontological foundation of services science: The general service model. In *Wirtschaftinformatik Proceedings 2011*.
14. Kim, Y. J., & Nam, K. (2009). Service systems and service innovation: Toward the theory of service systems. In *AMCIS 2009 Proceedings*.
15. Papazoglou, M. P., & Van Den Heuvel, W.-J. (2006). Service-oriented design and development methodology. *International Journal of Web Engineering and Technology, 2*(4), 412.
16. Kohlmann, F., Börner, R., & Alt, R. (2010). A framework for the design of service maps. In *AMCIS 2010*.
17. Papazoglou, M. P., Traverso, P., Dustdar, S., & Leymann, F. (2008). Service oriented computing: A research road map. *International Journal of Cooperative Information Systems, 17*(02), 223–255.
18. Khadka, R., Saeidi, A., Jansen, S., Hage, J., & Helms, R. (2011). An evaluation of service frameworks for the management of service ecosystems. In *PACIS 2011 Proceedings*.
19. Dai, H., & Salam, A. F. (2010). An integrative framework of service convenience, service consumption experience, and relational exchange in electronic mediated environment (EME). In *ICIS 2010 Proceedings*.
20. Glushko, R. J., & Tabas, L. (2009). Designing service systems by bridging the '"front stage"' and '"back stage"'. *Information Systems and e-Business Management, 7*(4), 407–427.
21. Gordijn, J., Yu, E., & van der Raadt, B. (2006). e-Service design using i* and e3value modeling. *IEEE Software, 23*(3), 26–33.
22. Motta, G., Barroero, T., & Telese, I. (2011). Design of performance aware service systems—A conceptual framework and a case study. In *2011 International Joint Conference on Service Sciences*.
23. Weigand, H., Johannesson, P., Andersson, B., & Bergholtz, M. (2009). Value-based service modeling and design: Toward a unified view of services. In *CAiSE 2009, LNCS 5565* (pp. 410–424).
24. Medaglia, R. (2011). Engaged scholarship in research on information technology in government. *Information, Communication & Society*, 1–14.
25. de Ven, A. H. V. (2007). *Engaged scholarship: A guide for organizational and social research*. Oxford University Press.
26. Mathiassen, L., & Nielsen, P. A. (2008). Engaged scholarship in IS research. *Scandinavian Journal of Information Systems, 20*(2), 3–20.
27. Baskerville, R. L., & Wood-Harper, A. T. (1998). Diversity in information systems action research methods. *European Journal of Information Systems, 7*, 90–107.
28. Comerio, M., Grega, S., Palmonari, M., & Viscusi, G. (2012). Alignment of service science and service oriented computing: A unified interpretative approach to service design and planning. In M. De Marco, D. Te'eni, V. Albano & S. Za (Eds.), *Information systems: Crossroads for organization, management, accounting and engineering* (pp. 519–526). Heidelberg: Physica.
29. Kaner, M., & Karni, R. (2007). Design of service systems using a knowledge-based approach. *Knowledge and Process Management, 14*(4), 260–274.
30. Viscusi, G., & Batini, C. (2010) 'Policy: The GovQual Methodology, the Italian case. Overview' and 'Tools: The GovQual Methodology, the Case of the eGovernment for Mediterranean Countries (eG4M)'. In Workshop E-Government tools in practice: How to

develop a sound implementation road map organised by the MENA-OECD Governance Programme with the Palestinian National Authority, Ramallah, 5–7 July 2010.

31. Viscusi, G., Batini, C., & Mecella, M. (2010). *Information systems for eGovernment: A quality-of-service perspective.* New York: Springer.
32. Batini, C., Viscusi, G., & Cherubini, D. (2009). GovQual: A quality driven methodology for E-Government project planning. *Government Information Quarterly, 26*(1), 106–117.
33. Viscusi, G., & Palmonari, M. (2008). IPAS: An ontology based approach to government to business service selection. In 19th International Workshop on *Database and Expert Systems Application, 2008. DEXA'08* (pp. 749–753).
34. Palmonari, M., Viscusi, G., & Batini, C. (2008). A semantic repository approach to improve the government to business relationship. *Data & Knowledge Engineering, 65*(3), 485–511.
35. Choucri, N., Maugis, V., Madnick, S., & Siegel, M. (2003). Global e-Readiness: for What? MIT Sloan School of Management, Paper 177.
36. Batini, C., Viscusi, G., & Castelli, M. (2013). Design on a societal scale: The case of e-Government strategic planning. In R. Baskerville, M. De Marco, & P. Spagnoletti (Eds.), *Designing organizational systems* (Vol. 1, pp. 267–283). Berlin Heidelberg: Springer.
37. Mylopoulos, J., Chung, L., & Yu, E. S. K. (1999). From object-oriented to goal-oriented requirements analysis. *Communications of the ACM, 42*(1), 31–37.
38. Rolland, C. (2007). Capturing system intentionality with maps. In J. Krogstie, A. L. Opdahl & S. Brinkkemper (Eds.) *Conceptual modelling in information systems engineering* (pp. 141–158). New York: Springer.
39. Zeithaml, V. A., Bitner, M. J., & Gremler, D. D. (2006). *Services marketing: Integrating customer focus across the firm.* New York: McGraw-Hill.
40. Aagesen, G., & Krogstie, J. (2011). Service delivery in transformational government: Model and scenarios. *Electronic Government, an International Journal, 8*(2/3), 242–258.
41. Kranz, M., Murmann, L., & Michahelles, F. (2013). Research in the large: Challenges for large-scale mobile application research—A case study about NFC adoption using gamification via an App Store. *IJMHCI, 5*(1).

Printed by Publishers' Graphics LLC